HOW TO SPARK CREATIVITY

CATALYTIC TECHNIQUES TO SPUR YOURSELF INTO
ACTION AND IMPLEMENT YOUR CREATIVE
PROCESS NOW

WISDOM UNIVERSITY

CONTENTS

Exclusive Offer

4 Bonuses + Free Access To ALL Our Upcoming Books!

Free Bonus #1

Our Bestseller
How To Train Your Thinking
Total Value: $9.99

If you're ready to take maximum control of your finances and career, then keep reading...

Here's just a fraction of what you'll discover inside:
- Why hard work has almost nothing to do with making money, and what the real secret to wealth is
- Why feeling like a failure is a great place to start your success story
- The way to gain world-beating levels of focus, even if you normally struggle to concentrate

★★★★★

"This book provides a wealth of information on how to improve your thinking and your life. It is difficult to summarize the information provided. When I tried, I found I was just listing the information provided on the contents page. To obtain the value provided in the book, you must not only read and understand the provided information, you must apply it to your life."

NealWC - Reviewed in the United States on July 16, 2023

"This is an inspirational read, a bit too brainy for me as I enjoy more fluid & inspirational reads. However, the author lays out the power of thought in a systematic way!"

Esther Dan - Reviewed in the United States on July 13, 2023

"This book offers clear and concise methods on how to think. I like that it provides helpful methods and examples about the task of thinking. An insightful read for sharpening your mind."

Demetrius - Reviewed in the United States on July 16, 2023

"Exactly as the title says, actionable steps to guide your thinking! Clear and concise."

Deirdre Hagar Virgillo - Reviewed in the United States on July 18, 2023

"This is a book that you will reference for many years to come. Very helpful and a brain changer in you everyday life, both personally and professionally. Enjoy!"

Skelly - Reviewed in the United States on July 6, 2023

Free Bonus #2

Our Bestseller
The Art Of Game Theory
Total Value: $9.99

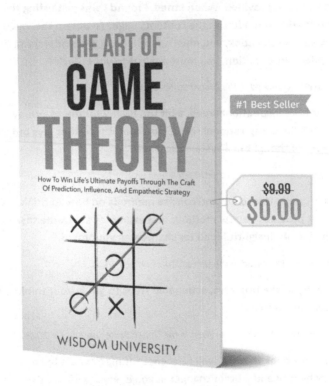

If Life is a game, what are the rules? And more importantly... Where are they written?

Here's just a fraction of what you'll discover inside:

- When does it pay to be a selfish player... and why you may need to go inside a prisoner's mind to find out
- How to recognize which game you're playing and turn the tables on your opponent... even if they appear to have the upper hand
- Why some games aren't worth playing and what you should do instead

"Thanks Wisdom University! This book offers simple strategies one can use to achieve things in your personal life. Anyone of average intelligence can read, understand and be in a position to enact the suggestions contained within."

David L. Jones - Reviewed in the United States on November 12, 2023

"Haven't finished it yet, but what I've gone through so far is just incredible! Another great job from this publisher!"

W. S. Jones - Reviewed in the United States on October 12, 2023

"A great book to help you through difficult and complex problems. It gets you to think differently about what you are dealing with. Highly recommend to both new and experienced problem solvers. You with think differently after reading this book."

Thom - Reviewed in the United States on October 18, 2023

"I like this book and how it simplifies complex ideas into something to use in everyday life. I am applying the concept and gaining a lot of clarity and insight."

Ola - Reviewed in the United States on October 18, 2023

"The book is an excellent introduction to game theory. The writing is clear, and the analysis is first-rate. Concrete, real-world examples of theory are presented, and both the ways in which game theory effectively models what actually happens in life is cogently evaluated. I also appreciate the attention paid to the ethical dimensions of applying game theory in many situations."

Amazon Customer - Reviewed in the United States on October 8, 2023

Free Bonus #3

Thinking Cheat Sheet
Break Your Thinking Patterns
Total Value: $4.99

Free Bonus #4

Thinking Sheet
Flex Your Wisdom Muscle
Total Value: $4.99

<u>A glimpse into what you'll discover inside:</u>

- How to expose the sneaky flaws in your thinking and what it takes to fix them (the included solutions are dead-simple)
- Dozens of foolproof strategies to make sound and regret-free decisions leading you to a life of certainty and fulfillment
- How to elevate your rationality to extraordinary levels (this will put you on a level with Bill Gates, Elon Musk and Warren Buffett)
- Hidden gems of wisdom to guide your thoughts and actions (gathered from the smartest minds of all time)

Bonus #5

Get ALL our upcoming books for FREE
(Yes, you've read that right)
Total Value: $199.80*

You'll get exclusive access to our books before they hit the online shelves and enjoy them for free.

Here's everything you get:

✓ How To Train Your Thinking eBook   ($9.99 Value)

✓ The Art Of Game Theory eBook   ($9.99 Value)

✓ Break Your Thinking Patterns Sheet   ($4.99 Value)

✓ Flex Your Wisdom Muscle Sheet   ($4.99 Value)

✓ All our upcoming eBooks   ($199.80* Value)

Total Value: $229.76

Take me to wisdom-university.net for my free bonuses!

(Or simply scan the code with your camera)

Scan Me

*If you download 20 of our books for free, this would equal a value of 199.80$

WHAT READER'S ARE SAYING ABOUT WISDOM UNIVERSITY

"Wisdom University embodies an innovative and progressive educational approach, expertly merging deep academic insights with contemporary learning techniques. Their books are not only insightful and captivating but also stand out for their emphasis on practical application, making them a valuable resource for both academic learning and real-world personal development."

—*Bryan Kornele, 55 years old, Software Engineer from the United States*

"Wisdom University's works provide a synthesis of different books giving a very good summary and resource of self-help topics. I have recommended them to someone who wanted to learn about a topic and in the least amount of time."

—Travvis Mahrer, BA in Philosphy, English Teacher in a foreign country

"I have most of the ebooks & audiobooks that Wisdom University has created. I prefer audiobooks as found on

Audible. The people comprising Wisdom University do an excellent job of providing quality personal development materials. They offer value for everyone interested in self-improvement."

—Neal Cheney, double major in Computer-Science & Mathematics, retired 25yrs USN (Nuclear Submarines) and retired Computer Programmer

"WU is a provider of books regarding mental models, thought processes, organizational systems, and other forms of mental optimization. The paradigmatic customer likely is to be someone in an early- to mid-career stage, looking to move up the ranks. Ultimately, though, the books could be of use to everyone from high school students to accomplished executives looking for ways to optimize and save time."

—Matthew Staples, 45, Texas (USA), Juris Doctor, Attorney

"I have been reading books from Wisdom University for a while now and have been impressed with the CONDENSED AND VALUABLE INFORMATION they contain. Reading these books allows me to LEARN INFORMATION QUICKLY AND EASILY, so I can put the knowledge to practice right away to improve myself and my life. I recommend it for busy people who don't have a LOT of time to read, but want to learn: Wisdom University gives you the opportunity to easily and quickly learn a lot of useful, practical information, which helps you have a better, more productive, successful, and happier life. It takes the information and wisdom of many books and distills and organizes the most useful and helpful information down into a smaller book, so you spend more time applying helpful information, rather than reading volumes of repetition and un-needed filler text.

—Dawn Campo, Degree in Human psychology and Business, Office administrator from Utah

"I'm a subscriber of Wisdom University for over a year now. I would recommend Wisdom University books to anyone who wants to improve their understanding of cognitive behavioural therapeutic principles."

—Sunil Punjabi, Maharashtra (India), 52, PhD, Psychologist

"I wanted to read some books about thinking and learning which have some depth. I can say "Wisdom University" is one of the most valuable and genuine brands I have ever seen. Their books are top-notch at kindle. I have read their books on learning, thinking, etc. & they are excellent. I would especially recommend their latest book "Think Like Da Vinci" to those who want to have brilliant & clear thinking."

—Sahil Zen, 20 years old from India, BSc student of Physics

"I came to know about Wisdom University from the Amazon Kindle. There were recommendations for some of the Wisdom University books. Found every book very interesting. I really loved it. Subscribed for the free material which was delivered right into my inbox. Since then, I have been a fan. I couldn't buy the books... since am in a situation. But as soon as I get a sufficient amount, I plan to purchase some nice titles that piqued my interest. I recommend the books to everybody who wants to live a life free from all sorts of mental blocks that reflect in real life. These books are definitely the lighthouse, especially for those crawling through the darkness of ignorance. I wish Wisdom University all the best."

—Girish Deshpande, India, 44, Master of Veterinary Science, working as an Agriculturist

INTRODUCTION

There's something that I already know is true about you. It doesn't matter if you're a teacher in your 30s with three kids, a newly single bank broker, a young musician, a successful entrepreneur, or a retired landscaper. You all have something in common.

I know this without ever having to speak a word to you or even look at you. You could be at any stage in your life, in any career path, and live anywhere in the world. This thing likely makes you feel not good enough to pursue the things you want to pursue. It's something that can feel embarrassing to admit. It's something that led you to pick up this book in the first place. This statement is true of *almost everyone*.

I know that you struggle with your creativity.

That might seem like a bold assumption, but here's the thing: we all do. Every single one of us, even the most creative people in the world, struggles to hone their creativity and make it shine when it counts. It's not as simple as switching it on and off; creativity is a fickle trait. We all possess creativity—at varying levels—but there is no foolproof method of activating creativity that works for everyone.

We hear stories all the time about people being struck with a bolt of inspiration and endless motivation and drive to materialize the vision. But in reality, this is rarely the case. Most of the time, creativity is fleeting and random. It can be easy to fall into a pattern of feeling creatively stuck, and before you know it, you have a creative block.

It can be difficult, almost shameful, to admit to struggling with activating your creativity because it is often spoken of as a trait that comes effortlessly and naturally. With traits like strength or intelligence, you can decide pretty easily when you want to use them. Yet, for creativity, it can sometimes feel like you can't get it to work no matter how hard you try.

What's the point, then, of reading a book about improving your creativity if there is no universal method of activating it? Well, just because there is no *universal* remedy doesn't mean you can't find what works for you. If there is one thing I can promise, it is that there is something out there that will bring out your creativity.

You may have creative skills but don't know how to best unleash them. Or perhaps you are seeking guidance, input, and inspiration on how to own and embody your own creativity and break free of typical routines. You might have gotten sidetracked from your creative passions by the demands of work, family, marriage, or any other of life's challenges. If any of these resonate, this book is for you.

In this book, you'll find science-based knowledge, strategies, and techniques distilled into digestible chapters. You'll meet other people who struggle with the same challenges to creativity and learn how they overcame even the greatest obstacles to their creativity. Along the way, you'll find practical tips, exercises, and activities to try and apply your new knowledge.

You have the potential within you to unleash the creativity that already exists. You *already* have abundant creativity, brilliant ideas, and the will to use them—all that's left is learning how to channel them by understanding your unique creative style and personal circumstances. The benefit of releasing your creativity is the fulfillment of your greatest creative ambitions and goals.

How do I know all of this? I've struggled with creativity myself. I hesitate to even put "struggle" in the past tense; the creative journey is ongoing and evolves just as you do. That's why it's so important to understand what works for you and be able to adapt when familiar solutions stop being as effective.

The greatest irony is that, in the process of writing this book about embodying your creativity, *I still faced obstacles to my creativity*. Lots of them. I struggled to find the motivation to write, not to judge my work before it had even been written, and to come up with interesting and engaging ideas. I had to remind myself that I am also part of the audience of this book because all creatives go through these same experiences.

I am a writer, printmaker, and creative who has spent much time developing my creative process. Finding out what works for me involved a lot of trial and error. I've had to adapt my creativity to academic environments, professional contexts, and personal projects while juggling all of life's other responsibilities.

In theory, all the ideas, thoughts, and research presented in this book will help you optimize your creativity. But in practice, things are always more complicated. I faced this truth when writing this book. I am imperfect, and I don't always follow my own advice or make the right choices in the moment. As a creative, I have to keep reminding myself that it's normal to go through periods of difficulty. I share this because I'm sure you feel the same way, and it's important to know that you never need to set an expectation of perfection when it comes to creativity. You're allowed to be messy, make mistakes, and experiment with new things.

This book isn't meant to be passively read and put back on the shelf. It's meant to spur you into action with diverse strategies and activities that you can implement in your creative process immediately. This book is for people who are serious about their commitment to creativity.

So, are you ready to learn more about how you can improve your creativity? Keep on reading. The first chapter will answer the question "what is creativity?" You may think you know the answer, but the concept of creativity is surprisingly hard to define.

S. Pinto

1

HOW TO START YOUR CREATIVE PURSUIT?

DECIPHER THE FUNDAMENTALS OF CREATIVITY TO IGNITE YOUR IMAGINATIVE THOUGHT PROCESS

In the third grade, my elementary school teacher would have us do a drawing exercise each day to practice being creative. "Just think outside of the box!" Ms. Stryker would proclaim, darting around the classroom as she looked over our shoulders at our burgeoning creations.

Lacking in illustration skills, I always struggled to materialize the visuals in my imagination onto the page. If I intended to draw a magnificent scene where a red-winged bird swooped over a glimmering city nightscape, I ended up with a blob of red above a series of misshapen rectangles.

Mostly, I ended up running out of time before any of my grand visions came to life on paper. Every time I felt that I had drawn a line out of place, I furiously erased it and began again until I felt that it was perfect. If what I created wasn't good, how could I call myself a creative person?

Ms. Stryker would leave encouraging comments on my drawings such as, *Keep it up! Try using your imagination*, and *You'll improve with practice.* These comments discouraged me even more.

I never understood how Ms. Stryker's metaphor of thinking outside the box would translate into improved creativity. If anything, I felt like my enjoyment of illustration decreased after seeing the finished drawings that paled in comparison to my talented peers. That whole school year, I continued to draw blobs and wonder how this exercise was helping my creativity.

I felt the most creative when I was writing. Something about the pencil scratching on paper made the scenes in my imagination come to life: stories about scuba diver escapades to locate chests of pearls and gold, fantastical flying creatures soaring through futuristic cityscapes, and quests through maze-like jungles flowed out of me effortlessly.

I didn't worry about whether each detail in my story was neatly wrapped up at the end or if I had misspelled words. I just let my imagination guide me and was delighted by the process of writing stories.

I intuitively knew how to be creative when I was writing. Why couldn't I translate the skill to my drawings?

One day, I finally gave up on making a perfect drawing and drew a dog kicking a soccer ball into a spinning vortex. I worried less about making each line perfect and finished the drawing without thinking too much about the result. Ms. Stryker's feedback changed. "What a creative idea," she wrote on my paper in red ink.

When I finally stopped setting myself such a high standard for *acceptable* creativity, I was able to actually enjoy what I was doing and allow myself the freedom to create without bounds.

I intrinsically knew *how* to be creative, almost without trying. As children, we all did. But I would venture a guess to say that we weren't actually sure what creativity was.

Though the word creativity exists in our everyday language, most people would be hard-pressed to provide a precise definition for the word on the spot. Is creativity the state of... being creative? Is it thinking outside of the box? Is it coming up with ideas? Is it breaking existing rules? Beyond cultural cliches, the meaning of creativity is nebulous and unclear.

So, what exactly is creativity? In this chapter, we will explore a few definitions of creativity and overview different conceptions of what creativity is. I will discuss common challenges to being creative and some of the many benefits of creativity. I'll summarize key points from major creativity thinkers and researchers to give you a broad understanding of *what creativity is* and offer three actionable tasks to help you apply what you've learned and kickstart your way to being more creative.

Defining Creativity

Let's get into it. So, creativity is such a popular concept that even a third grader could tell you what it is. Yet it's so nebulous of a concept that it's hard to pin down its precise meaning.

Creativity is essential to the decision-making process, to innovative thinking, to art and culture, and even to scientific pursuits. Perhaps it is because creativity is so ingrained within us that we find it difficult to separate from other traits. Some even say that it is creativity that makes us human.

Dictionary definitions of the word are surprisingly unhelpful. Take Merriam-Webster's definition of creativity, which describes it as "the quality of being creative."[1] Below this definition, Merriam-Webster also lists some synonyms of creativity: cleverness, imaginativeness, originality, invention, and ingenuity. These synonyms give us a better idea of what creativity is and signal similar qualities, but still do not quite give us an understanding of what creativity means.

Beyond simple definitions of the word, creativity takes several shapes. Writer Kyle Bernier theorizes that creativity comes in two types: tangible creativity, which is producing something physical in the world, and thought creativity, which is creativity that occurs within the mind.[2]

Of course, these two types overlap and thought creativity often leads to tangible creativity.

Let's see what creativity researchers have to say about the definition of creativity. Earlier articles about creativity pinpoint it as an *idea* or *concept* rather than an object, describing the word creativity as a "noun naming the phenomenon in which a person communicates a new concept" (p. 305).[3]

A 2022 book about creativity describes creativity as "an *embodiment* of the things that you are, beyond a knowledge of facts or a cluster of skills."[4] Much like the previous definition, we seem to think of creativity as having almost magical properties that transcend concrete and measurable characteristics.

According to researchers in the *Creativity Research Journal,* the current standard definition of creativity is that "creativity requires both originality and effectiveness."[5] Yet, like most fields of study, this definition is constantly disputed and revised.

The authors of this paper note that originality on its own isn't enough to constitute creativity: "a truly random process will often generate something that is merely original."[6] This definition tells us that creativity must serve some purpose; it must be an effective solution to a problem. Though you may not always feel as though you are trying to solve a problem when you are being creative, you can think of this effectiveness as bringing something into being. For instance, if you illustrate a scene from your imagination, your illustration is an effective representation of this thought through a visual mode. In other words, you have effectively communicated an idea through creative expression.

Most definitions from creativity experts take similar approaches to defining creativity, using words such as *surprise, novelty*, and *value* to pin down the meaning of this word.

But for someone like you, the reader of this book, definitions like the ones above may not reflect what creativity means for *you*. You're not a research subject or a lexicographer and you may not even have a problem you're actively looking to solve—you're just looking for practical tips to improve your creativity. You may be looking to improve your creativity to help you at work or simply to reconnect with your creative practice.

What if we could roll all these definitions into one definition of creativity that is focused on you as the individual and what it means to be creative in practice? In this case, you might think of creativity simply as *imaginative and curious creation while connecting to the self*. Although this definition is not official, it acknowledges our purpose in this book: inspiring your personal creativity!

This is not to say that the previous definitions are redundant or impractical. It is also important to recognize the scholarly and historical work being done on creativity so that you have a well-rounded picture of what creativity is. In fact, the work of these researchers and writers will inform much of the content in this book.

Later chapters in this book will cover some of the brain mechanics of creativity in greater depth, but for now, this discussion of definitions will provide you with a base understanding of what I mean when I talk about creativity.

Differentiating Creativity From Similar Concepts

How is creativity different from craft or artistry? Creativity is so often associated with the development of skills that come along with it that many consider them to be synonymous. Though it overlaps with concepts like artistry, talent, and imagination, creativity is its own distinct concept. Now that we've gone over some definitions of what creativity is, we can talk about what it *isn't*.

You can differentiate creativity from these concepts like artistry, talent, knowledge, and imagination by thinking of it as the mental process behind the skills you develop. For example, if you are a painter, creativity is the force that compels you to create your paintings, but artistry is the level of skill and competence that you acquire as you become a more skilled painter.

Similarly, you might be naturally talented at painting, but perhaps you can only emulate the styles and content of other painters rather than creating your own original process. Your knowledge might be of different brush techniques, but you might not be able to apply them creatively. In this case, you may combine your talent and knowledge of different painting techniques to produce your paintings rather than engaging in a creative process to make something that is entirely your own.

The most similar concepts are creativity and imagination. Again, these two concepts certainly overlap. I would argue that it is impossible to have true creativity without also having imagination. Imagination allows you to conceptualize and dream up concepts, but creativity is the practical process of bringing these imagined concepts, ideas, and dreams into the world.

Yet imagination is still different from creativity, you can have a highly active imagination but fail to transform it into a tangible form by using your creativity. For example, you could imagine a grand scene in your mind but be unable to create a painting, story, or other forms of expression from it.

Creativity often involves at least one of these other characteristics, yet it is a distinct entity. Creativity permeates almost all fields, workplaces, art practices, and other totally mundane aspects of our lives. Cooking, for instance, is a highly creative endeavor! Have you ever had to improvise your dinner based on the ingredients you had at hand? That is an example of creativity in everyday life.

Creativity is not necessarily about being technically skilled, uniquely talented, or artistically gifted. It's easy to compare yourself to artists or amateur creators with an innate knack for art and feel like you'll never measure up. You can be terrible at art and still be creative. Creativity is for *everyone*.

You probably practice creativity all the time without even realizing it! As with cooking, there are many ways that you are creative everyday that *may or may not* include artistry, imagination, talent, and knowledge. Have you ever come up with a clever game or activity for your children to play while stuck in line at the store? Doodled on a sticky note while talking on the phone? Or maybe you've proposed an alternative plan or strategy in a work meeting? Though you might not think of these things as creative practice, they are! Everyone is capable of creativity; it is only a matter of nurturing the creative state of mind to increase your creative capacity. The ability to be creative is already within you.

Why Is Creativity Important?

Hayley is a young waitress in a trendy downtown restaurant by day and a singer by night. Every Friday night, Hayley and her band play gigs at a local bar, making just enough money to cover transportation expenses and upkeep for their equipment.

Hayley's friends often ask her why she had never wanted to be a professional singer; for her, singing allowed her to creatively express herself with her voice and have cathartic release from stressful emotions. Besides, she wasn't the most talented singer. For her, singing allowed her to access the benefits of creativity without the pressure of having to be exceptionally talented at her chosen activity.

The day after a performance, Hayley feels like she is on top of the world. Her confidence increases, she feels happier, and she is more capable of dealing with the day-to-day stress of her life. She may not be a Grammy-nominated performer, but for her, the creative benefits of singing are all she needs to feel fulfilled.

It's a well-known fact that being creative has incredibly positive impacts on cognitive health for individuals. Beyond the personal, creativity is also "a major source of innovation, growth, adaptability, and resilience" for society at large.[7]

Creativity impacts you on both an individual level and a social level. If it is nurtured and regularly exercised, creativity offers countless benefits that will help you in your day-to-day life. Here are just a few:

- Creativity encourages out-of-the-box thinking that challenges our minds to explore new ideas, concepts, and questions.
- Creativity allows you to express yourself and your individuality.
- Creativity can relieve stress and help you process complex emotions.
- Creativity can help you build community with others and create interpersonal connections.

Yet despite these obvious benefits, many of us find it difficult to practice creativity because we're tired, can't find the time, or simply can't access the inspired parts of ourselves that drive us to be creative.

Even if we can find the time and energy to be creative, many people find that their inner critic disparages anything they produce or stops them from creating altogether.

These challenges stop people from accessing the many benefits of creativity because they are too scared to be bad at it and often feel like being creative is pointless if they cannot make a profit from what they produce.

Yet the results of your creativity are also an incredibly meaningful contribution to the world. Though it might not seem like it, each pen stroke, colored canvas, or hand-spun ceramic is a unique artifact that tells a story about your life as a human at the moment it was created. Though it may not seem special to you, it might survive and become an impactful piece of evidence for future generations and even researchers. Your creativity is important, not only for you individually but also for the story of humanity.

I will unpack this idea throughout the book so that you can cultivate your creativity and unlearn that you don't need to be good at what you do to be creative.

Creativity's many benefits to your well-being extend to your mental health. Because of its practicality, creativity can also be a form of therapy. When you're engaging in a creative activity, you're allowing your mind to process complex emotions and make sense of the world around you. Many therapy and psychology practitioners use art therapy with their patients. Using creativity as therapy is also something you can learn to do on your own (but keep going to therapy, too!).

It may be helpful to think of creativity as a form of discovery and invention. Instead of creativity as the process of making a masterpiece, try approaching it with the same attitude as you would an experiment. The product—a discovery or invention—is the result of the experiment. You can't predict what the outcome will be in advance! Even if you have a hypothesis, the results may be entirely different than what you had expected.

Creativity may be something you do by yourself or something that you share with others. If you've ever participated in a choir or written a story in response to a piece of art that inspired you, you've already experienced shared creativity.

And that's the thing—you don't need to paint like Van Gogh for your creativity to develop. Creativity comes with practice, patience, and curiosity. You're probably being more creative by doodling on that sticky note while you're on a work call than fretting over the proportions of your intricate work-in-progress that is collecting dust in your home.

Action Steps

Now it's time to apply what you've learned with a series of short exercises and tasks to get you thinking about creativity. I know, I know—you just want to keep reading! But taking the time to reflect on what you've learned and applying some of these skills will immediately put you on the path to increasing your creative capacity.

1. Write out some of your thoughts on creativity. What is your existing definition of the word? What does it look like to be creative? How might these ideas be unhelpful to your own creative process and inhibit your creativity?

2. What are your intentions when you create? Do you have a certain amount of time you want to devote, or are you interested in finishing a certain project?

3. Try making some bad art on purpose. Take a blank sheet of paper and a medium of your choice (pen, pencil, paint, etc.) and give yourself 10 minutes to create. Afterward, write a short reflection about the process. What does it feel like to let go of being good at something?

Moving On

As I did, you may think back to your childhood and remember what it was like to be effortlessly creative and have no fear of judgment (by yourself or others).

My teacher Ms. Stryker wasn't wrong to have us practice being creative with a daily drawing practice. In fact, though I may not have understood it at the time, this approach encouraged me to try a medium I wasn't familiar with and allowed me to make mistakes as I figured things out. It allowed me to fail and keep going—something that, as a perfectionist, made me deeply uncomfortable.

As an adult, I still struggle with wanting to be good at art to do it. Yet I often think back to Ms. Stryker's class. What I know now is that failure is a natural byproduct of creativity. The more you embrace it, the easier it will become to let your creativity free.

Though I didn't realize it at the time, I was the most creative when I was not stressed about being *good* at what I was doing. This skill came to me naturally as a writer, but when I experimented with different activities like drawing, I felt that my creative output needed to be good.

Now that you're familiar with the definition of creativity, its benefits, and some different types of creativity, you might be wondering how best to hone your own creativity.

In the next chapter, we will review the creative process and how to set up your own personalized creativity process.

Chapter Summary

- Many creativity researchers associate creativity with originality, surprise, and imagination.
- You likely engage in creativity every day even if you don't realize it.
- You can be bad at art and still be a creative person.
- Creativity challenges the mind, increases your self-expression, and reduces feelings of stress and anxiety.

2

DISCOVER YOUR CREATIVE PERSONA

PRACTICAL STRATEGIESTO DECODE YOUR
DISTINCT ARTISTIC PATH TO ELEVATE YOUR
CREATIVITY

Back To The "Wood" Old Days

To Anthony, a 43-year-old accountant, the days of practicing woodworking are long gone. In his late teens and early 20s, Anthony took woodworking electives at his high school and college and gained a deep love for the craft. He was pretty good at it, too—in his many years of practice, he had made everything from a desk to use for doing homework to a set of oak patio chairs for his mother's backyard.

Anthony loved woodworking because it allowed him to detach himself from the intense mental challenges of his finance and business courses. Though he enjoyed being analytical and learning about finance, using his hands to create items from wood was a welcome break from his studies. Feeling the grain beneath his fingertips as he cut wood for his projects gave him a mental release from the world.

Woodworking made Anthony feel creative and ready to take on any challenge at school. It was the only time that he was free to pursue personal projects. He began every woodworking session by laying out his materials and tools, sketching out a plan for his project in his notebook, and queuing up his favorite techno music in his headphones.

Anthony landed a job as a Junior Accountant at a reputable accounting firm after graduating from college. He moved out of his hometown and into a bigger city and began working 9+ hours a day and commuting to and from work on the subway. Though he liked his new job, Anthony missed taking woodworking classes and grieved the access to woodworking studios that enrollment at the college had allowed him.

But Anthony kept his head down and continued to work for the firm, excelling in his role and accepting promotion after promotion. And before he knew it, Anthony had met his wife, and they started a family together. Between work and raising his children, he had little time for himself.

After several years, the loss of his creative time began to take a toll on Anthony's well-being. He noticed that he had more difficulty concentrating at work and all he could do in the evenings after work was sit and watch TV until it was time to sleep. It had been more than a decade since Anthony had picked up any of his woodworking tools.

He decided to join a local woodworking studio. Filled with excitement, he was almost giddy the first night that he visited the studio after work. Yet when he arrived, he found that he had no idea what he should make.

He told himself that he would start simply; he would make a chair. After all, it had been quite some time since he last used any woodworking tools. That first night, he crafted a decent dining chair but was disappointed that he did not experience the same inspired fulfillment that he used to feel while woodworking. His next few visits to the woodworking studio ended similarly.

Anthony recognized that he needed to incorporate creative time into his life again but felt that he had lost all his creativity in the years since he had been in school. Though he was able to find time for woodworking, the creative spark was gone.

Is there a way to restore lost creativity?

I'll let you in on a little secret: Finding your creative process is key to improving your overall creativity. Many people get stuck in a rut because they just "don't feel creative." This is a common sentiment among creatives, yet it is surprisingly simple to remedy.

Lacking a creative process can lead to an artist's block, feeling uninspired, and hating the results of the work that you do produce. The creative process is all about silencing the critic within you that stops you from creating before you can even start.

The nature of creativity is to make connections between existing ideas in innovative ways, and Anthony's woodworking process allowed him to stimulate his mind. Creativity stems from cognitive and emotional processes and curiosity about the world that leads to fulfillment.

You might think of the creative process as solving a puzzle.[1] The process is investigative, curious, and the outcome is a natural conclusion to the process. You might even say that the outcome is an accident of the process.

Crafting a creative process can help reverse these issues by tricking your brain into a ritual that subconsciously tells your brain to let go of the inner critic and release your fearless creativity. Everyone has their own creative personality! Identifying your own creative personality and process will help you restore the feeling that you've lost your creativity.

How Do You Develop A Creative Process?

It took me a long time to figure out my own creative process. I spent several years feeling like I had lost the ability to write creatively. Every time I sat down to write, the blank page taunted me. I would flip back through old poems and stories I had written and feel ashamed that I couldn't conjure up the same imaginative drive that I used to have. Was I a fraud? Had those moments of creativity been coincidental?

Even after I had learned about the benefits of a creative process, I was skeptical. How would a certain string of actions and environmental changes help me to be creative?

Being in graduate school forced me to take these words of advice seriously. There's no time for writer's block when you've got three 6000-word essays due at the end of each semester. I began experimenting with how I approached my writing sessions.

Everyone's creative process is going to look different, but sometimes it's helpful to see someone else's process for ideas on how you can make your own. Here is a good starter creative process and how it can work in practice for you.

Freeing Up Mental Space

A major obstacle to many people's creativity is being distracted by anxieties and fears, remembering things you need to do later, and feeling like your thoughts are all over the place

Have you ever been about to sit down for some focused creative time when your brain decides to remind you that you need to do your laundry, prep your lunch for tomorrow, or make that doctor's appointment? Me too. These thoughts take up a ton of mental space and make it difficult to be creative.

To help me get rid of pesky thoughts like these, I like to do what is sometimes called a "brain dump," an activity where you take a piece of paper and write down anything and everything that comes to mind before you begin your creative practice. The point of a brain dump is to create a space where those thoughts can be recorded so that you aren't worried about forgetting something important.

Try spending 10 minutes before your next creative session writing down any thought, idea, or worry that comes to your mind. It doesn't matter how irrelevant or innocuous these thoughts are; I keep this piece of paper beside me as I write so that any time a distracting thought arises, I can write it down and be assured that it will be there for me to return to later.

Doing a brain dump is a crucial part of my creative process. It allows me to reassure my brain that all the important stuff will be taken care of *after* my creative time. If you find yourself struggling to clear your mind when embarking on a creative project, try a brain dump to free up some of your mental space.

Changing Your Environment

If you often do your creative work at home but find that you can't focus for long, you may need to change the environment in which you do creative work.

During the pandemic, I struggled to do creative work within my home. Because I rarely left the house, my space shrunk to fit the needs of working from home, pursuing hobbies, and continuing to be a space where I cooked and took care of my basic needs. Because it became the place where I spent 90% of my time, I was always distracted by chores that needed to be done or just ended up laying in the comfort of my bed when I had planned to do some art. I suspect that many people have been in the same boat.

Changing up your workspace can improve your ability to be creative. This is because our environment affects our behavior, mood, concentration, and more. For some, the ambient noise of a cafe or communal office environment aids the process of creative workflow; for others, the quietness of a library or home workspace is what does the trick.

Finding your optimal environment can increase your creative productivity. One study that looked at the effect of environment on creativity for 409 employees found that even adjusting ergonomic factors in the workplace "foster[s] the creativity of employees at any level in the organisation."[2]

For me, this meant sometimes working from the nearby library or taking the time to rearrange my workspace at home to feel new and different. Even though I was living in a tiny studio apartment, I would move my desk to different areas of the room and experiment with space dividers, lighting, and furniture orientation. You'd be surprised at how different it feels to work at your desk when you've changed the colors of your lights and are pointing at a blank wall instead of out the window.

If you can't change your workspace at home, try working in a different area. This might look like taking your sketchbook to the park or making a makeshift studio on the table of your favorite cafe. You might have to get imaginative with how you do this depending on your preferred creative practice, but the point of changing your environment is just to experiment with somewhere new.

<u>Incorporating Ritual</u>

Developing a ritual to do before your creative time can help train your brain to enter a creative headspace.

Rituals have immensely helped me plan out creative time and ensure that I will be in the right headspace to get into my creative flow.

The trick is to make your ritual consistent and unique to your creative practice. For example, you don't want your creative ritual to be similar to your bedtime routine!

Personally, my ritual begins by tidying up my workspace to remove clutter, wiping down my work surface, and preparing any materials I will need while working. Next, I will make myself a beverage (usually tea or coffee). The process of preparing my beverage helps ground me as I turn my mind toward my creative endeavor. Once I have my beverage, I sit down at my workspace and light a candle to have with me at my desk, signifying the start of my creative session. Finally, I take out a piece of paper to begin my brain dump from point #1.

My ritual is simple and short; these steps never take me more than half an hour to complete. Yet they make all the difference to my creativity. After my creativity ritual, my mind feels clear and ready to be creative.

Reducing Or Replacing Sensory Stimuli

It may seem obvious, but many of the barriers to your creativity come from distractions from your senses. This can be anything from hearing TV noise in another room of your house to fighting off pangs of hunger while you're trying to focus.

I find that visual distractions and noise are my major issues when I am trying to be creative. To combat these sensory distractions, I've learned to dim the lights around me and use noise-canceling devices to reduce the amount of sound I can hear around me. Reducing the sensory input from these two sources has been a game changer for me—I can finally focus on what is in front of me instead of getting distracted by the world around me.

However, some people may find that the opposite is true for them. Many of my creative friends *require* there to be noise or visual stimulation around them in order to be creative. One study suggests that noise can be beneficial for your creativity, stating that "a moderate level of noise not only enhances creative production but also leads to greater adoption of innovative products."[3]

If that's the case for you, figure out what sensory input you need to be creative and put yourself in an environment where you are exposed to those things.

Putting My Phone Away

Okay, I'm sure you saw this one coming, but removing your phone *really does help with your creative process*. Most apps on your phone are designed to capture your attention and keep you focused on the screen instead of what you should really be doing—or what you really *want* to be doing.

One study acknowledges the widely accepted attitude that phones may "hav[e] a negative impact on our ability to think, remember, pay attention, and regulate emotion," all aspects of your cognition that influence your creative ability.[4] Though the study concludes that the empirical research to support this sentiment is still limited and evolving alongside technology, the data we do have now and how our phones have "become increasingly interlaced with our cognitive functioning" provide good reason to be mindful of how it shapes our daily creative practices.

Does that mean that you can freely use your phone without any impact on your creativity?

There's certainly a time and place for time on your phone, but when you're trying to have creative time, having your phone around might be affecting your ability to connect with your inner creative. Unless, of course, your creative practice directly involves your phone—in that case, keep on!

But if you're feeling distracted by your phone while trying to be creative, I suggest placing your phone in a different room—or at least out of your direct line of vision—before starting your creative time. This will help you focus on your task at hand without being distracted by notifications, text messages, and emails.

If you need your phone nearby, at least make sure that it's turned over and on silent mode. I put my phone on "do not disturb" to make sure that no attention-grabbing notifications reach the screen while I am engaging in creative work.

<u>Time Blocking</u>

I personally find it very beneficial to loosely structure my creative time. Techniques like time blocking and the Pomodoro technique can all be useful to give yourself defined periods of creativity with space to take short breaks and rest your mind.

Time blocking is a technique that involves scheduling tasks or activities into "blocks" of time based on how long you think they will take to complete. For example, you could block out two hours of painting time each evening in your calendar.

Similarly, the Pomodoro technique calls for you to work in creative "bursts," usually around 25 minutes of focused creative time followed by a five-minute break. You repeat this interval four times before taking a longer break. You can set a timer to help you keep track of time or find a Pomodoro tracker to do it for you—there are lots of free Pomodoro tools online.

A creative flow that works for me is 45 minutes of focused creative time where I let go of my inner judgment and allow myself to create freely, no matter how "bad" I think it is at the moment. After the 45 minutes, I leave my work for the moment and get up to stretch, drink water, and wander around for 15 minutes. This short break refreshes me and allows me to continue again. Generally, I do 3-5 of these intervals.

For some, applying any kind of structure to your creative time will hurt your process rather than help it. If leaving your time completely free of any structure works best for you, that is totally fine, too.

Action Steps

Try these two exercises to experiment with your creative process:

1. Reflect On What Distracts You From Your Creativity.

What senses tend to distract you during creative time? Are you annoyed by clothing that is too tight, noise from other parts of your home, or distracting visual stimulation around your working area?

Take a moment to reflect on what sensory input may need to be changed when you want to be creative. (If you can't think of anything right now, you might also wait to do this activity until the next time you try to be creative and just notice what comes up for you!)

When you've figured out some things that tend to distract you, brainstorm ways to reduce these distractions. If you're bothered by the tightness or discomfort of your clothes, you might try changing into loose, comfortable clothing. If you get distracted by noise, try using earplugs or listening to white noise. If it's visual stimulation that is the problem, rearrange your workspace or try dimming the lights.

It may take some time to figure out exactly what distracts you. Be patient and keep a log! It might take a while, but eventually, you will find what works for you.

2. Test Out A Creative Process.

While you were reading this chapter, did anything stand out to you? Perhaps you remembered that going for a brisk walk or having your cup of coffee in the morning helps you get into a creative mood. Maybe you know that you feel the most inspired when your favorite genre of music is playing. Write down a few ideas for your creative process and test them next time you do something creative.

If nothing resonated with you, I encourage you to experiment. Try something new each time you make time for creativity until you find something that sticks.

Moving On

Unable to find the same joy in woodworking as he previously used to, Anthony consulted a new friend at the studio for advice on rediscovering his creativity.

His friend Myra advised him to think less about the result of woodworking and more about how he felt during the process. She reminded him that he was still easing back into his passion and it might take some time to reconnect with that part of himself.

"You should try to reflect on what it was that made woodworking so enjoyable for you back then," she suggests. "What was it like back then? What has changed?"

Anthony eventually realized that the reason that he was struggling to rediscover his creativity in woodworking was that he was missing the routine he had when he was younger.

Remember how part of his woodworking routine when he was younger was to lay out his materials and tools, make a written plan for his project, and set up his headphones to play his favorite music? It turns out that these steps helped set Anthony up for creative success.

Anthony decides to experiment. He prioritizes the setup time for his woodworking sessions, making sure to ruminate on his plan for each project and find music to listen to that he enjoys. He savors the process of arranging his materials before starting and takes his time to finish each piece instead of rushing through the process.

To his surprise, he begins enjoying the woodworking process again before he even finishes his next piece. Instead of deliberating over every cut of wood, he trusts the process and allows himself to make mistakes and take risks before getting to the result. After a few months of practicing this creative process, Anthony's creative drive is restored.

Experimenting with a creative process helped Anthony rediscover his love for an old passion. Oftentimes, we can become too focused on the production or result of our creative efforts and not enough on the routines, habits, and behaviors that enable our creativity. The creative process that works for you will be unique and tailored to your own needs and preferences.

In the next chapter, we will delve further into figuring out what kind of creative you are and how best to support your creative journey.

Chapter Summary

- Developing an effective creative process will help you improve your overall creativity.
- A good creative process is consistent and distinct; it does not resemble any other routine in your life.
- Figuring out what sensory needs you have will help you modify your environment to facilitate quality creative time.

3

WHAT'S YOUR CREATIVE VIBE?

A BRIEF GUIDE TO IDENTIFYING YOUR ARTISTIC
STRENGTHS TO ELEVATE YOUR INNOVATIVE
PURSUITS

An Unexpected Accolade

Tammy has never thought of herself as a creative person. She grew up loving 1000-piece puzzles, Rubik's cubes, and model airplanes, which she assembled herself. In school, she was praised for her abilities in math and sciences which led her to her career as an engineer. She had never cared much for painting, drawing, and other activities traditionally associated with creativity. In her mandatory high school art class, she secretly did math problems when the teacher wasn't looking.

However, in her job as a traffic engineer, Tammy is praised for her innovation and technical expertise. She has a reputation around the office for her hand-drawn road concepts that set her firm's proposals apart from the pack and that feature inventive solutions to problems like road widening, speed management, and traffic control.

Tammy loves her work and considers it an extremely precise and calculated vocation. Her desk is covered with scribbled calculations, measurements, and sticky note reminders.

Every year at the Christmas work party, Tammy's firm hands out awards to stand-out employees for exceptional work and dedication. To her surprise, Tammy receives the award for Creative Excellence in Engineering this year. Her coworkers flood her with praise and congratulations on her achievement. But if she is honest, she is perplexed by why she received this award.

She catches her supervisor's eye toward the end of the night and approaches her to inquire about the award.

"I don't mean to be ungrateful. I am really honored to receive this award. But I just don't understand," she explains. "My work doesn't involve creativity—it involves applied mathematics and technical knowledge. Was there some kind of mistake?"

Her supervisor chuckles kindly, touching her hand to her heart.

"Tammy, just because your work is mathematical doesn't mean it can't also be creative," she says. "This wasn't a mistake. Sure, your mathematical and technical abilities are impressive. It's a given in this kind of career. Everyone in this room excels at those kinds of capabilities—but not everyone here can apply them the way that you do. Not everyone knows how to use those skills to design original solutions to complex problems.

You might not think of it as creativity, but it certainly is."

The next week, Tammy places her award on her desk and the silver words "Creative Excellence in Engineering" gleam back at her. Her supervisor's words echo in her brain: *Just because your work is mathematical doesn't mean it can't also be creative.* Perhaps her conception of a creative as someone who did visual art and had ideas that came from emotions instead of logic was incomplete.

Though the common archetype of creativity might be what Tammy is picturing, there are many different types of creatives. In this chapter, we will discuss the various types of creatives using questions for you to reflect on and frameworks from creativity researchers. You can decide the type of creative you view yourself to be.

Identifying the kind of creative you are will help you refine your creative process and tune into the types of activities, processes, and methods that will help you enhance your creativity.

Identifying Your Creative Strengths

Like Tammy, you may not consider yourself conventionally creative. If your creativity is strongest in areas like computer programming, engineering, mathematics, science, or even athletics, the word creative might not be an adjective you often use to describe yourself. Others may view you as logical and analytical—yet neither of these things is exclusive to creativity!

Even if you are conventionally creative, identifying your strengths can help you to have a stronger sense of how you thrive creatively. Painters, illustrators, dancers, actors, and others may also identify with types of creativity that are misconstrued to be un-creative, such as being methodical or analytical.

To reflect on your creative strengths, consider asking yourself the following questions:

Do you consider yourself imaginative?

Do you consider yourself artistic?

Do you consider yourself crafty?

Do you consider yourself manually skilled?

Do you consider yourself mathematical?

Do you consider yourself scientific?

Where else do your creative strengths lie?

While answering these questions, think about the kinds of activities and hobbies that you feel you are generally proficient in. You may recall the graceful movement you embodied when you did ballet in your youth, the ease with which you learned auto repair skills in your high school mechanics class, or your knack for repurposing scrap materials into beautiful home decor.

Of course, this list is not exhaustive—don't worry if these attributes do not resonate with you. There are many different possibilities for the types of creative that you may be. In the action steps at the end of this chapter, I'll ask you a few more questions to help you identify your unique mix of creative attributes.

If you knit or embroider in your free time, you may consider yourself crafty. Hey, even if your hobby is planning and designing architectural masterpieces, you have a unique mix of creative attributes!

Tammy, for instance, did not think of herself as imaginative or creative until she had a conversation with her supervisor. While she certainly resonated with being mathematical and scientific, she did not come to think of herself as artistic or imaginative until further reflection on her work.

She thought about the conceptual drawings she made by hand and the mathematics she regularly applied to address and regulate complicated traffic scenarios. She recalled the deep state of focus she entered when working on a new project where she had to conceptualize traffic patterns and redesign important pieces of infrastructure.

Creativity comes in many forms. You can engage in virtually any activity creatively. However, what creativity *feels* like—or, you might say, how the creative process feels—looks different for everyone.

Creative Subtypes By Process

According to A. Dietrich (2019), creatives may be divided into three sub-types: "a deliberate mode, a spontaneous mode, and a flow mode."[1] We might think of creatives operating within these states of mind. Identifying which process works best for you will help determine which type of creative you are.

Of course, for most people there will be some overlap between these types or they may find that they switch between them. However, you may find that your creativity gravitates to one of these types over the others.

There are other ways to imagine different types of creativity. Since creativity is an abstract concept, these types are not meant to be definitive and stringent categorizations.

Dietrich describes the three subtypes as follows:

- **Deliberate Mode:** the creative process relies upon deliberate and repeated trial and error. This mode is associated with conscious choice, effort, and planning.
- **Spontaneous Mode:** allowing creativity to occur spontaneously and without clear intention or process. This mode is associated with effortlessness, surprise, and lack of intention.
- **Flow Mode:** practicing creativity through physical motion and beyond the conscious state of mind. This mode is associated with action, effortlessness, and intense concentration.

You might think of the deliberate mode as experimenting with the effects of darkroom photograph development until you reach a desirable outcome; the spontaneous mode as creating a painting based on a dream you had; and the flow mode as becoming so immersed in dance that you lose track of time.

You can likely remember a time when you experienced one of these states while engaging in a creative activity. You may have experienced the deliberate mode when you tried developing a new cranberry-muffin recipe and tried multiple iterations with minor tweaks, the spontaneous mode when you acted on a creative inspiration that came to you, and the flow mode when you hunkered down to finish a project before a tight deadline.

The flow state is considered to be desirable but highly elusive. Athletes are thought to have among the highest levels of flow, but studies also show that musicians experience it with a high frequency as well.[2]

The end of this chapter will suggest a few activities to try and experience each of these creative modes for yourself. Do any of these situations sound familiar to you? It can be hard to identify these moments of creativity in your life, especially if you are unconventionally creative, so let's help you identify areas in your life that are filled with creativity that you may not have thought of as such.

Where Can You Find Creativity In Your Life?

For you, creativity might not be something you engage with in your free time. Perhaps, like Tammy, your creativity is found within your vocation.

Let's take a look at another character who displays unconventional creativity. If you've never thought of yourself as a creative person, you may identify with this character, and his story may help you figure out what sort of creative you are.

Tammy's husband, Nelson, is a professional soccer coach for a nationally ranked college team. In his work, he develops training plans and team bonding exercises for his athletes. In his 15-year career, he has won multiple awards and recognition for his coaching expertise. Though his athletes might not always love the decisions he makes for them, he always has the team's best interest at heart and always strives to improve their game performance with new strategies and skills.

Nelson attended Tammy's work party and watched her receive the award for creativity. Like Tammy, his initial reaction was one of perplexity until Tammy explained the conversation that she had with her supervisor. Hearing that Tammy's work could be considered creative made him reevaluate his own profession.

Nelson considers all the hours he's spent studying exceptional World Cup games and Premier League matches and translating the best plays into strategies for his own team. He has spent hours at his desk evaluating each player's strengths and talents and how to best leverage them in a game with so much unpredictability and chance.

He knows that, to most people, it's the athletes that determine the outcome of a game by manipulating the ball into the net. But Nelson knows that professional soccer is much more than kicking around a ball; it requires months of practice, strategy, and coordination to make a team successful. Last season, a play that he developed and had his athletes practice led to the moment that his striker scored the winning goal.

Nelson realizes that his work *does* involve creativity. He must imagine and anticipate infinite outcomes of a match; concoct activities and speeches to make his team feel connected to each other, inspired to work together, and willing to push through the pain and physical strain of the sport; and solve any common issues that have cost his team wins.

As a creative, Nelson is *imaginative, analytical,* and *resourceful.* When his team is discouraged after a loss, he knows what to say to rile them together for the next game. When he identifies a common pattern that leads to his team repeatedly losing possession of the ball, he strategizes ways of avoiding the same outcome next time.

"Tammy, this is changing the way I look at my job," Nelson gushes. "I never looked at this work as being creative in any way. But now I see just how much creativity impacts my work and how I can use this knowledge to improve my work even more. I can lean into my creative strengths to motivate my players and devise clever game plans that will give us an advantage during matches."

Though, like Tammy, Nelson had never considered himself to be a creative person, upon reflection he realizes just how much he *is* creative in his everyday life, and how it is because of creativity that he excels in his vocation.

Action Steps

Now that you've learned about a few different types of creativity, try out these steps to apply them to your own life.

1. Write A List Or Brainstorm Some Of Your Creative Strengths.

Here are a few prompts to get you started: In which areas do you excel creatively? Can you think of examples of projects or tasks you've worked on where your creativity has significantly helped you accomplish something? In what ways are you unconventionally creative? Can you list 3-5 adjectives that describe the kind of creative that you are? In which areas do you feel you are the *least* creative, and why? Can you think of a complex or unusual problem in your life that you solved by coming up with a creative solution?

2. Think About How Creativity Already Exists In Your Life.

Creativity permeates almost every aspect of your life. It's likely that at least some elements of your job involve creativity. You may also have hobbies or activities you do in your life that involve creativity. If you don't paint, knit, or draw, that doesn't mean that none of your activities lack creativity–think hard about how creativity shows up in the activities that you already engage in. For example, do you enjoy shopping for antiques to decorate your home? The process of selecting antiques and designing your space constitutes an example of creativity! If you're stuck, you might have to spend some time reflecting on where creativity shows up in your life; being able to identify it will help you understand how to bring creativity more into your life. It could be as simple as the morning crossword you fill out every morning!

3. What Creative Process(es) Work Best For You?

Look back at the section in this chapter titled "Creative Subtypes By Process." I challenge you to try engaging in each creative process for half an hour with these three activities:

- **The deliberate mode**. Use a pen and paper to draw different versions of a simple object such as a chair for thirty minutes. Did you learn anything in the process? Did trying different techniques teach you anything about the drawing process?
- **The spontaneous mode.** Find a piece of paper and a medium that you can mark the paper with (paint, pencils, or pens will work for this activity). Spend the next thirty minutes marking up the paper without intentionally planning or thinking about what image you are

creating. At the end of the thirty minutes, reflect on what you have created. How did the process feel? Is there anything unexpected or surprising about what you created?

- **The flow mode.** Spend thirty minutes moving to any type of music that you enjoy. Focus on the feeling of moving your body and how this movement responds to the sound input. It doesn't have to be good! Try not to judge how you look or how your body moves. How did this activity make you feel? Did you enter a rhythm of movement that felt effortless? Has your state of mind changed in response to this activity?

After you've intentionally tried all three modes, was there one that felt the most natural to you? Did any of them feel familiar? Try implementing anything you learned into your creative practice.

Moving On

Both Tammy and Nelson had never considered themselves to be conventionally creative until others pointed out these traits within them, prompting them to reflect on how they practice creativity in their daily lives.

Tammy and Nelson can identify experiences with each different mode of creativity when they are working. For Tammy, the deliberate mode is a process that she had unknowingly been engaging with in her career for years.

As she makes calculations for her road designs, she uses trial and error to find the best solution for each problem.

For Nelson and his players, the flow state is where they find most of their creativity. During games, they call this being "in the zone," a state where their body moves almost without conscious thought and they drown out the noise of the busy stadium.

Everyone's creative type is different and trying out other processes will help you enhance your creative strengths. In the next chapter, we'll discuss the components of creativity in more detail.

Chapter Summary

- Most people engage in creative activities in their daily lives even if they don't realize it.
- Creatives come in many forms, including unconventional types such as those that are mathematically or scientifically creative.
- There are different processes of creativity, such as the deliberate mode, the spontaneous mode, and the flow mode.

4

THE TAPESTRY OF CREATIVE IMPRINT

UNDERSTAND THE THREADS OF CREATIVITY TO INFLUENCE YOUR ARTISTIC BRILLIANCE

A Magical Creative Space

As a child, I used to enjoy writing from a makeshift desk in my closet. I crammed a child-sized table and chair into a small nook in my closet with my clothing hanging above me and wrote poetry and prose in the dim, enclosed space.

Something about being confined in a small space lacking the usual distractions in my room helped me focus. I had a regular-sized desk in my room, but I often found that when I sat down to write, I would quickly become distracted by nearby toys, unread books, or other objects. But in the closet, all I could really see was the paper in front of me. My imagination did the rest.

You may recall a similar spot that had an almost magical effect on your creativity: the cafe down the street with a window spot and *just* the right amount of ambient noise, a library carrel tucked away in the corner, or your art studio where the energy of your peers creating beside you spurred on your own inspiration.

Small details like location, stimulus, and support from peers are all components of creativity that greatly impact your creative performance.

This chapter will cover the components of creativity, drawn from Mihaly Csikszentmihalyi in his book *Creativity: Flow and the Psychology of Discovery and Invention,*[1] and how you can enhance these components to improve your overall creativity.

Component 1: Existing Domain

Your existing knowledge constitutes one component of creativity. An existing domain—an area of knowledge that you are already familiar with—is the smallest component of creativity. Your knowledge of ballet, pottery, martial arts, music composition, science, tap dancing, and more might be considered a domain. You might gain this knowledge from your community or at school, or it may come from your experiences in the world.

This component is a vital part of creativity. It is less about what you are producing by being creative and more about the existing knowledge that leads to your creativity. Your domain is likely in an area that inspires you to *be* creative. Have you ever read a great novel and thought "this gave me a great idea for a book!" Or have you ever conducted an experiment in the lab that sparked an idea for a related study? These are examples of domains in action.

Everyone will have countless domains in which they have varying amounts of knowledge. Each person's unique interests and experiences will also inform their domains. And, of course, there is a ton of crossover between domains. You may find that your interest in cooking leads you to develop knowledge about different cuisines around the world and, by extension, the history and traditions of these cultures that led to the creation of these dishes.

In my personal example from childhood, writing was my domain. I learned different forms of writing, such as a short story or a sonnet. I learned in school how to create rhymes and play with vowel sounds to create assonance. This knowledge about different forms of writing is an example of domains.

Yet domains on their own do not constitute creativity; rather, it is how we approach them that leads to creative output. This approach to domains is **the act**.

Component 2: The Act

The act is the component of creativity where the individual approaches their domain in a novel way, combines areas of a domain, or otherwise manipulates their domains to create something new.

You can think of the act as taking something that is familiar or traditional and making it new. Marla, a pop singer, loves listening to songs by The Beatles. She knows almost all their songs by heart. She decides that she is going to record a cover of herself singing "Here Comes the Sun" for an upcoming album. Knowing that the song has been covered many times by many different artists, Marla decides to put her own spin on it, using her unique vocal range to make the song more upbeat and lively.

The result is a cover that blends Marla's pop style with the beloved melody. She speeds up the beat and introduces layered background vocals to add depth. Though recognizable by its lyrics and tune, Marla has transformed "Here Comes the Sun" into something entirely new.

Marla uses her existing domains (her knowledge of music and singing and her love of The Beatles) and approaches an old tune in a new way to creatively make the song her own. In this way, Marla's actions represent two of the creative components.

So far, we've spoken about creativity as it exists within an individual. Both domain and act are components that can be isolated to just one person. Yet we are all impacted by those around us, and the components of creativity extend beyond just our knowledge and approaches to creative output. The next component will consider an aspect of creativity related to those around us.

Component 3: The Field

Our next component of creativity moves beyond individual actions and knowledge into how those around us can influence and inform our creativity. This component, called the field, represents our peers and those who engage in similar creative endeavors to us.

In academic settings, the field may be understood as a subgroup within your area of study. If you're a philosophy professor, your field may be made up of scholars who research the philosophy of Immanuel Kant. Your colleague's field may be those who specialize in metaphysics. You both share a common domain—the foundational elements of philosophy—but the peers that make up each field are different.

However, the field can be made up of multiple layers. In the previous example, I described sub-groups of philosophy as fields. Yet we could also consider all scholars of philosophy as a field separate from those studying psychology, history, or political science. Of course, there are often overlaps between each of these components.

When Marla considered the other covers that singers have made of "Here Comes the Sun," she was influenced by the field because she had heard other covers of the song and responded to the pop genre by melding the two in a unique way. Those who engage in the genre of pop music would also constitute a field, and the changes and trends in this field influence how Marla approaches her own music.

Your field may be people that you actually know in real life or it might be more abstract. In the action steps at the end of this chapter, I will suggest a reflection exercise so that you can figure out what your field looks like.

Component 4: Surroundings

The fourth component of creativity is your surroundings. Your surroundings include where you work and live, and how these are structured reflects your needs and your tastes. At this point, I might sound like a broken record, but *everyone is different*; evaluate your needs and desires and find what works for you!

One aspect of your surroundings is the larger area in which you live. This might be an urban center, a rural location, or a small town, but your surroundings also include your home, your workplace, and your favorite hangout spots. Your surroundings can inspire your creativity and create the conditions for you to be creative.

Another aspect of your surroundings is the area where you like to engage in creative activities. This could be your art studio, kitchen table, or favorite cafe.

It's important to have access to surroundings that allow you to immerse yourself in a creative activity and maintain concentration for an extended period.

Yet it is also important for your surroundings to offer you stimulation and novelty to carry you forward in your creative endeavors. If you have a space in your home where you like to be creative, it should be filled with objects that help you pursue your creative goals and minimize distractions. Curating a space with objects and ambience that works for you will serve your creative practice.

You don't need a designated space at home or even a cafe near you to have meaningful surroundings. For many people, being outside in nature is enough to inspire creativity. Your favorite place to create may be at your local park or a spot near the river by your house. It might be the sound of flowing water or the melody of chirping birds that activates your creativity.

Our surroundings are usually so familiar to us that we don't take the time to consider how they impact our creativity. However, they have a massive impact on our emotions and motivation.

Component 5: Culture

Our final component of creativity is the largest and most abstract of them all: culture. Culture is a component of creativity that significantly impacts your creative output. It affects the kinds of creative techniques and activities you are exposed to and the types of thoughts and ideas you have.

Though I might not have realized it as a child, my culture had a considerable impact on the content and type of things I created. I grew up in North America in an urban city and went to public school where I learned how to write very early on. I had access to public libraries where I was able to read many different books. I also had loose ties to my family's heritage, which meant that I was exposed to other languages and customs.

Factors like religion, socioeconomic class, geolocation, and social values may change how culture impacts your creativity. Growing up, I had friends who went to Cantonese school on the weekends to learn about their own language and culture. In college, I met an artist that practiced a traditional weaving method from her Haida background.

Culture impacts us in ways that we may not even recognize, and therefore, culture influences the ways that our creativity comes into play. Even if you are not consciously aware of it, your culture impacts your creative output, the language that you think in, and your knowledge and perspective about the world.

Leaning into your cultural context can inspire you and deepen your creative practice.

Action Steps

1. Identify each component of creativity in your context. What are your domains of knowledge? How do your approach and actions differ accordingly? Which fields do

you operate in? What are you surrounded by? How does your culture influence you?

2. Understanding these components of creativity, how might you modify your creative practice? For example, would exposure to a new domain or field spark your creativity? Consider your surroundings. How do they positively or negatively impact your creative practice? How about exposing yourself to a new culture by learning from a close friend?

3. Consider who makes up your field. If you are taking dance classes at a local studio, your field may be made up of those immediately around you who you can observe and learn from. If you are a writer, perhaps you have never met those in your field in person–the authors of the books that you take inspiration from may be your field.

If you're stuck, try these prompts:

- Who do I know in real life who is practicing this creative output?
- What media or resources have I consulted to learn about this activity?
- Who inspires me or is doing similar work in this creative activity?
- It's okay if you come up with multiple answers or have a lot of overlap!

Chapter Summary

- There are five components of creativity: the existing domain, act, field, surroundings, and culture. These components simultaneously influence your creative output.
- Components of creativity are not just within an individual. The world around you will impact your creativity whether or not you are aware of it.
- You may have more control over some components of creativity than others. You can choose to gain knowledge in a new domain, but you can't change the culture in which you grew up (though you can still learn about new cultures!).

5

WHERE INTELLECT MEETS CREATIVITY

HOW THE SYNERGY OF HUMAN INTELLIGENCE AND CREATIVE PRACTICE REFINE YOUR THOUGHT PROCESS

In creating the famous statue of David, what domains did the sculptor Michelangelo possess? What skills did he use to carve the fine lines of a human body from stone and visualize the elements of his creation before it came into being? The skills and talents of this sculptor can certainly be considered numerous, but this chapter will delve into several types of domains and how they impact your creativity.

In the previous chapter, we discussed the domain as a component of creativity that relates to your existing knowledge. I will further develop this concept to explain how your skills, traits, and knowledge underlie your creative performance and why learning is so important to developing your creative practice.

Domains are a set of representations or understandings underlying your comprehension of a specific area of knowledge and performance of the tasks associated with that domain. For instance, a painter's knowledge of the craft will include the execution of specific brushstroke techniques, the ability to mix colors accurately, and so on, which are part of the domain.

If you are especially skilled in a domain, you might consider yourself talented or gifted in that area. Researchers like Howard Gardner have theorized that every individual has a distinct combination of domains in which they excel.

In Howard Gardner's book *Frames of Mind: The Theory of Multiple Intelligences*, the author explains that "there is persuasive evidence for the existence of several relatively autonomous human intellectual competences," otherwise referred to as human intelligences (p. 8).[1] Though Gardner uses the word "intelligences" to describe areas in which individuals excel, this framework helpfully illustrates the concept of domains as areas of knowledge in which a person might have natural excellence or learned skill. Gardner's book, first published in 1983 but has had multiple reprints, has been highly influential in the field of education.

Now, you may be thinking, what does intelligence have to do with creativity? Because intelligence is characterized by being able to learn and problem solve, it has a direct connection to creativity. Gardner's theory of multiple intelligences has direct applications to creativity.

A common misconception about the popular idea of intelligence is that it is a static, uniform trait. The word is largely used to describe those who excel in academic contexts. Many people may even think of being intelligent and being smart as the same thing—but they're not! Whereas smart is the quality of learning quickly and being able to apply knowledge, intelligence is commonly defined as a greater ability to *learn* and problem solve.

Acknowledging that there is no definitive method to characterize every aspect of intelligence, Gardner sets out to break down what constitutes an intelligence and a rough sketch of the different types of intelligences. In the following quote, Gardner explains the limitations of his theory:

There is not, and there can never be, a single irrefutable and universally accepted list of human intelligences … Why, then, proceed along this precarious path at all? Because there is a need for a better classification of human intellectual competences than we have now … and perhaps above all, because it seems within our grasp to come up with a list of intellectual strengths that will prove useful for a wide range of researchers and practitioners … to communicate more effectively about this curiously seductive entity called the intellect. (p. 64)[2]

Despite the recognition that there is no perfect system to describe intelligence, Gardner proposes that the merit in understanding and categorizing it helps not only researchers to understand it further but also individuals to hone their skills.

Gardner thus proposes that we can break down intelligence into seven types: linguistic intelligence, musical intelligence, logical-mathematical intelligence, spatial intelligence, bodily-kinesthetic intelligence, and intrapersonal and interpersonal intelligence. Furthermore, each person has their own unique combination of these areas of intelligence. Those areas of intelligence where a person excels might be considered talents.

Many of these categories may seem quite straightforward, but let's dive deeper into each type of intelligence and tease out the nuances of each category.

Mapping Intelligences

Linguistic Intelligence

Linguistic intelligence refers to the ability to understand and manipulate sounds, rhythms, and meanings of words to shape language. In Gardner's view, this intelligence is most associated with poets and influential speakers. Individuals who excel in linguistic intelligence are highly attuned to the meaning of words and can manipulate them to create the impact that they desire. They are adept at understanding how the connotations of a word change its significance in a sentence—changing even the tiniest word can alter the gravitas of the sentence!

Gardner notes that people in positions with great influence (leaders, politicians, or public speakers) are often linguistically intelligent. They know what and how to say things to people that produce the outcome or emotion that they desire.

Musical Intelligence

Recognizing and producing rhythm, pitch, and timbre are markers of those who possess musical intelligence. If you can tune a violin with ease or pick out a stray note in a song, you possess musical intelligence. Individuals who are musically intelligent are able to express themselves easily through music.

Musically intelligent individuals seem to pick up new instruments effortlessly and can analyze and identify each distinct harmony or pattern within a piece of music.

Though this intelligence may seem similar to those with linguistic intelligence, Gardner notes that the part of the brain that activates when engaging in a musical activity is different from the part that activates when engaging in a linguistic activity.

Logical-Mathematical Intelligence

Logical-mathematical intelligence involves recognizing numerical and logical patterns and producing chains of reasoning from these observations. People with this intelligence are highly rational and capable of assimilating complex ideas and problems with step-by-step calculations.

Gardner suggests that individuals with this intelligence are skilled in analyzing and assessing quantities of objects and reordering them in their minds.

Though you might immediately think of mathematical geniuses as having this intelligence, which they certainly do, people in the field of formal logic in philosophy are also intelligent in this area. If you've ever seen a philosopher of logic create a proof that looks like a mathematical equation, that's why! The mathematician and logician have in common their ability to mentally categorize chains of patterns and represent their conclusions in an ordered fashion.

Spatial Intelligence

Spatial intelligence is the ability to understand the visual-spatial world and transformations within that world by using visual data to design or move through a space. People with this kind of intelligence are often able to visualize objects or spaces accurately in their minds.

Someone with this intelligence could be asked to picture a complex geometric shape in their mind and easily rotate it to different perspectives, describing how the shape's orientation has changed in the process.

People with this intelligence may be adept in navigation, designing interior or exterior spaces, mechanical tasks, or even performing surgery. Each task requires the individual to accurately conceptualize a space or object and manipulate objects or move their bodies so that the space or object changes to fulfill a desired goal.

Gardner explains that this ability may translate to an individual being able to recreate an object or space with a drawing to represent elements precisely as they appear.

Bodily-Kinesthetic Intelligence

A graceful ballet dancer, an Olympic gymnast, and a potter all have one thing in common: their ability to control the movements of their body with exactness and precision. Bodily-kinesthetic intelligence is having careful control of your body movements, such as being able to balance on a narrow surface or navigate a tricky obstacle.

People with this intelligence are generally able to have control of fine motor movements as well as larger movements requiring more strength or dexterity. In fact, you might think of this intelligence as being the *opposite* of clumsy.

Within the brain, movement control comes from the motor cortex. A ballerina's ability to move their limbs into an arabesque is the same as the potter, who moves minuscule muscles in their fingers to shape clay.

Interestingly, Gardner also claims that actors often possess this intelligence. To mime, he explains, requires careful manipulation of the body to perform an action without the help of physical objects. Imagine the classic image of a mime flattening their hands against an imaginary wall. Surely it takes exceptional control of the hands to create the optical illusion of a wall in thin air when no such structure exists!

Interpersonal Intelligence

Classified by Gardner as personal intelligence, interpersonal intelligence is the social ability to respond appropriately to the feelings, moods, and motivations of others. People with this intelligence can detect and respond to emotions within other people and act accordingly. Those who are intelligent in this way are highly attuned to others.

Interpersonally intelligent individuals can easily pick up on and understand others' moods and use this information to guide or influence them. Therapists and caretakers, Gardner suggests, are highly skilled in this area.

Intrapersonal Intelligence

Intrapersonal intelligence is understanding your own feelings, moods, and motivations, with assessing accurately your strengths and weaknesses, and with drawing upon such knowledge to guide your behavior. Those who are intrapersonally intelligent are highly introspective and reflective. They deeply understand their own emotional state and can identify the thoughts and feelings within themselves that guide their actions. Gardner considers this intelligence an information-processing capability directed inward, at the self, instead of outward at others. Being able to identify emotions and their causes within yourself allows you to adapt to new circumstances and explain your state to others.

Naturalist Intelligence

Our final intelligence is naturalist intelligence. Naturalist intelligence is the ability to recognize, categorize, and draw inferences about features of the environment and the organisms within it. This intelligence was not included in the initial publication of the book; Gardner later added it to his categorization of intelligences to describe individuals with a particular affinity for the natural world.

Individuals with this intelligence have a keen sense of patterns in the environment and identify relationships between organisms and their ecosystems. This intelligence allows the individual to understand their environment better and navigate the surroundings.

Intelligence And Creativity: What's The Connection?

Most people have some competence in each of Gardner's proposed intelligence areas; however, as mentioned, the level at which an individual excels in each area is different for everyone. Domains, or what Gardner has called intelligences, impact creativity by allowing individuals to apply their skillset and knowledge to a new endeavor.

Some of these intelligences may seem confusing to apply to creativity. For instance, how might interpersonal intelligences be creative? Well, a director of a movie must use their interpersonal intelligence to identify the states of their actors and support staff, decide how best to organize them, and provide feedback and instruction to create a successful production. The process of applying this interpersonal intelligence requires creativity to bring the production into being.

A sculptor, for instance, may be highly skilled in the areas of bodily-kinesthetic intelligence, visual-spatial intelligence, and intrapersonal intelligence. Creating a physical structure requires the sculptor to control the movements of their hands and body to manipulate the sculpting material. Sculptors are also required to visualize and manipulate space to transform it into the desired shape and be in touch with their inner state to translate the desired meaning and emotion into their creation. That's not to say that the sculptor lacks competency in other areas, too!

The connection between creativity and what we have called both domain and intelligence is its translation into production. One theory of creativity called the Amusement Park Theory (APT) model of creativity helps us visualize this process. APT uses an amusement park as an analogy for the creative process.[3] We can use this analogy in discussing the sculptor to explain how the theory works.

APT suggests that there is both generality and specificity within creativity that allows it to operate. The most specific, the micro-domain level, refers to skills that are unique to each domain whereas general creativity refers to creative skills that cross multiple domains.

First, you have initial requirements to arrive at the amusement park, such as transportation, which in the creative process might be your motivation to engage in an activity or your materials to perform the activity. For a sculptor, this may be your clay and sculpting tools, or your workspace. The specific amusement park you decide to visit represents your general thematic areas such as arts, sciences, or athletics. Within this general theme are specific locations in the amusement park that make up your domains, which might be dance, painting, or another activity. These domains are further divided into micro-domains (the specific rides you choose), representing the tasks or activities you may engage with in each domain, such as shaping your sculpting clay or carving the final details of your piece.

Individuals may be naturally skilled in one domain, but they can also develop their expertise in another domain with practice. To use the APT metaphor, you might initially visit a waterpark and gain familiarity with each activity in this domain before deciding to switch to an aquarium and developing the knowledge of each activity in that domain. For example, writing is a domain within the artistic/verbal area, and biology, chemistry, and physics within the math/science area. At a more granular level, poetry is the micro-domain within the writing domain, and nuclear energy within the physics domain. For a sculptor, you may specialize in a certain type of sculpting or use certain materials.

Creativity, then, occurs when one's domain and intelligence are applied to a project in a novel way. The steady hand of the sculptor must possess multiple capabilities and combine them in a new way in order for them to be creative.

Action Steps

1. Review Gardner's framework of seven intelligences. In which areas do you feel the most competent? Where do you feel the weakest? Were there any areas of intelligence that surprised you or you may not have considered?

2. Reflect on how the knowledge of these creative domains might shift your creative practice. Which areas might you strengthen to develop your skill in your chosen creative practice? How will you develop those areas? For example, if you think that improving your bodily-kinesthetic intelligence might improve your skills as a dancer, what steps will you take to develop this area? Implementing a balancing exercise routine? Improving your physical fitness? Making a goal to stretch for fifteen minutes a day? Devise a plan to improve the domains that you think will improve your creative practice.

Moving On

You may not have associated your areas of intelligence with your creative practice prior to this chapter, but each area in which you possess skills adds to your competencies in your chosen creative endeavor. In fact, many of the world's most creative people are multi-talented! The more information and skills that you pick up from different domains, the more they will impact other areas and improve your creativity.

Areas that you might consider completely irrelevant to your practice might actually have the most impact on your creativity. For example, if you are a writer, taking an illustration class may teach you visualization techniques that help you imagine and articulate scenes with increased attention to detail.

In the next chapter, we'll take a look at how the brain behaves when engaging in creative activity and discuss further how learning new skills can increase your creative capacity.

Chapter Summary

- According to Howard Gardner, there are seven areas of intelligences: linguistic intelligence, musical intelligence, logical-mathematical intelligence, visual-spatial intelligence, bodily-kinesthetic intelligence, and intrapersonal and interpersonal intelligence. Though these areas may overlap, each individual has their own unique profile of intelligences.
- Your creativity is influenced by the domains in which you are competent. Domains can be learned or may exist in an individual naturally.
- Domains can be looked at as both general and specific. At a general level, your relevant skills may overlap between domains whereas at the micro level, your skills may be specific to one micro domain.

- Learning a skill in a new area can teach you skills that unexpectedly transfer into your chosen creative area. Try new things, and you'll be surprised at how it improves your creative process!

6

NEURAL PATHWAYS OF CREATIVITY

UNDERSTANDING THE VARIOUS NETWORKS OF
THE HUMAN BRAIN THAT DRIVE YOUR
CREATIVE THOUGHT PROCESS

Prodigy Or Practiced Pro?

Francine, a French immigrant to America and mother to her 9-year-old daughter Amelie, notices that her daughter has learned English exceptionally quickly since they moved to America four years ago. Francine speaks basic English, enough to navigate life as an American and conduct her small business as a baker. When they first moved, she had taught Amelie simple phrases such as "where is the bathroom" and how to respond to questions about her name and age so that when Amelie started school, she could communicate with her teachers and peers. Francine worries that her daughter will struggle to keep up in school in a new language.

Because Francine works long hours at the bakery, she also hires a nanny to look after Amelie after school. The nanny she hires, named Maria, speaks both English and Spanish. While looking after Amelie, she often puts on her favorite Spanish shows on TV for them to watch together.

To Francine's surprise and delight, Amelie's progress in English far surpasses her own in just two years of living in America. Now, her daughter speaks English almost as well as her native-born friends! In public, Amelie translates difficult words for her mother with ease. Though Francine has taken intensive English classes since she first decided to move to America years ago, she just can't match Amelie's rapid progress.

Furthermore, Amelie has even picked up conversational Spanish through her time with Maria! Francine often overhears Amelie and Maria interacting in Spanish as she returns home from work. In just a few short years, Amelie has picked up two new languages before Francine can even master one. Plus, Amelie is still developing her native language as she matures.

Amelie also seems to excel in creative writing and has written short stories and poems in all three languages. Her teachers praise her ability to imagine exciting storylines and plot twists in her school assignments.

Francine is astonished by her child's many abilities. Has she raised a prodigy, or is there some other explanation for Amelie's rapid learning? How can we explain the phenomenon of Amelie's linguistic and scholastic achievements?

Neuroplasticity And Creativity

The answer lies in the inner workings of the brain.

Did you know that your brain behaves differently when you are being creative? More and more research is coming out describing how the brain reacts when we engage in a creative activity.

You may have heard of the term neuroplasticity before, which describes the creation of new neural networks in your brain that impact memory and learning. Every time you learn a new skill or problem solve an issue, your brain creates new neural networks using your experiences and information you receive in your environment.

The Encyclopaedia Britannica defines neuroplasticity as the "capacity of neurons and neural networks in the brain to change their connections and behavior in response to new information, sensory stimulation, development, damage, or dysfunction."[1]

Neuroplasticity offers an explanation for Amelie's many learned languages since moving to America and why Francine has had more trouble learning English than Amelie. Humans have the highest levels of neuroplasticity in childhood, but that doesn't mean that it stops when you reach adulthood. Nevertheless, these networks can be more difficult to create as you age. This is why it is easier to learn a new skill or pick up a new language in your childhood.

But you can still create neural networks as an adult, and they are extremely beneficial not only for your creativity but also for your well-being. You can actually *rewire* your brain using neuroplasticity to become more creative!

For Amelie, the simple act of moving to a new country changed the environment and stimulus that her brain received. She was exposed to new languages on a daily basis with opportunities to practice and apply the new knowledge. Her brain automatically began creating new neural networks in response to the change in environment. Because she was able to practice these skills every day, these neural networks were strengthened over time.

For adults, encouraging neuroplasticity can be more difficult because we have spent years strengthening our existing neural pathways. Yet it is not impossible to create new ones. Think of the age-old saying "practice makes perfect"! With repeated attempts at a new skill or learning experience, you can make new neural pathways and reroute existing ones.

So how can you consciously use neuroplasticity to your creative advantage? Your neuroplasticity is not something that you can dramatically increase overnight, but you can put in consistent effort to improve its function. Here are five consistent habits you can adopt to increase your neuroplasticity over time:

1. Learn a new instrument or language. Both language learning and music activate a similar part of the brain

thought to increase neuroplasticity. Though Francine's progress with language learning is slower than her daughter's, learning a new language is certainly creating new neural pathways in her brain.

2. Engage in regular physical activity. Physical activity in virtually any form stimulates the brain and encourages brain function. Exercise, especially a combination of aerobic and resistance exercises, has been found to boost neuroplasticity in the brain.[2] Various studies have found improvements "in cognitive domains including attention, processing speed and working memory are greater following a combination of aerobic and resistance training compared to either form of training alone."[3]

3. According to one study, foods high in omega-3 fatty acids (such as fish, nuts, and seeds), foods containing curcumin (such as turmeric), and foods high in resveratrol (such as grapes) all increase neuroplasticity and brain function.[4] Increasing or implementing these foods in your diet may improve your brain neuroplasticity. If you suspect you may be lacking these dietary components, try speaking to your physician about how you can incorporate them into your diet.

4. Play a game. This one might seem too good to be true, but engaging in a mentally stimulating challenge such as a difficult puzzle, a board game, a game of chess, or another challenging activity could actually increase neuroplasticity because of the problem-solving tasks involved. One study claims that it improves skills like

communication, cooperation, creativity, and critical thinking.[5]

5. Read a challenging book. It's time for a trip to the library! The focus and mental concentration involved in reading a challenging book requires you to engage your memory and analysis skills, in turn improving your brain function. Your reading this book right now is a good sign that you already practice this habit. If novels aren't your thing, you can achieve a similar effect by reading long-form news articles, non-fiction books, or experimenting with alternative modalities such as audiobooks.

Regularly practicing these five activities will improve your neuroplasticity over time. As adults, we often fall into routines and habits and spend less time learning new things than we did in our youth. Consciously putting in the effort to learn new things will help you break away from routine and develop new neural networks in your brain.

Learning new things can make you more creative by teaching you new skills and allowing you to see things from a new perspective. Try out any of these five habits (or more than one!) for a month and see the difference it makes in your creativity.

The Three Major Brain Networks

Now that you've learned about how the brain can change itself, it's important to understand *how* the brain functions when you are being creative. There are three major networks in the brain that are working at all times—even right now as you are reading this book! These networks are the default mode network, executive network, and salience network. Each network has to do with a different brain function, though they are all interconnected. Let's take a closer look at each network.[6]

The Default Mode Network

Have you ever found yourself distracted by thoughts of the future rather than being focused on the task at hand? This is the default mode network in action. Associated with daydreaming and imagination, the DMN is active when you aren't—that is to say that it is most active in moments of rest and when you are not focused on a specific task or goal.

You can think of this network as what goes on when daydreaming at work or zoning out on your commute home. This network is thought to encourage reflection and introspection on your emotions and experiences as well as producing creative ideas. DMN allows your brain to wander and produce thoughts and ideas unconsciously instead of choosing thoughts for consideration.

The Executive Network

The executive network is your brain's state when you are actively focused on a task or goal. Think of the last time that you were intensely engaged in an activity. This could be anything from completing a ten-lap run around the track to writing an essay speedily or completing an assignment that is due the next day.

When the executive network is activated, you experience fewer distracting thoughts and ideas. In this state, you exercise control over your thoughts and concentrate your focus on an activity. The executive network might be considered the "hard work" state of mind as you actively focus your attention on a difficult or challenging task. As you focus on reading this book, your executive network will activate; however, your brain will likely wander from time to time as DMN brings you in and out of focus.

Whenever you actively engage in a creative activity, your brain is in the executive network. The experience of losing track of time or feeling lost in the moment while being creative is an indication that this network is activated.

The Salient Mode Network

The salient mode network, or salience network, is involved in perceiving and filtering stimuli around you. In essence, the salient network selects what stimuli around you are significant. A loud noise, for instance, would activate this network.

The salient mode network also regulates your emotional reactions to the stimuli around you. Depending on the source of the loud noise that you heard, you may become upset or fearful if your brain perceives a threat, or you may shift to another network if your brain decides that the sound is not an indication of immediate danger.

Network Connections

These three networks also play a role when it comes to creativity. The interplay between these networks is what brings creativity alive. One study suggests that highly creative people possess the ability to activate these networks simultaneously.[7]

For example, Amelie found herself daydreaming one day at school during silent reading. The book she was reading gave her a great idea for her own story! Her brain shifts from focused reading—the executive network—to daydreaming about her own idea for a book—the default mode network. As she was daydreaming, her teacher called for the class to wrap up their reading, snapping her out of her reverie—the salience network. Although Amelie was not aware of the changes in any of these mode networks, they nonetheless ran in the background as she went about her day.

If Amelie were to decide that she wants to write the story she daydreamed about, she would have to focus on the task, activating the executive network. It's likely, though, that throughout the process, she will become distracted by her own thoughts as the default mode network comes on and off. Her salience network would monitor her environment for any changes that might need her immediate attention.

Understanding when and why your brain shifts between networks can help you streamline your creative process. Managing distractions can help you execute the production of your creative ideas, but all these networks play a part in the creative process. Though we often think of distractions as unhelpful, they can be extremely productive.

Many people have a similar experience when they step away from a problem or task to complete another activity such as a shower. During this resting state, their mind is free to make unconscious associations and links between ideas and experiences. This can lead to an "A-HA!" moment of revelation or breakthrough where the resting brain makes a connection that solves a problem that the focused brain couldn't. This is why many people say that their best ideas happen while they are in the shower!

Understanding the connections between these brain networks can help you the next time you feel creatively stuck or encounter a problem you feel like you cannot solve. Instead of forcing yourself to focus and problem solve, allow yourself to rest for a short amount of time. Take a walk in your neighborhood or close your eyes for a few minutes. You might even make yourself a snack and mindfully sit down to eat it.

This technique will work best if you limit the number of unnecessary distractions around you and let your brain wander. Of course, some distractions are unavoidable and can even be beneficial, but many distractions take us away from our creative practice. Identify which distractions can be removed or managed. Letting your mind daydream is unavoidable and can even help the creative process, but the barrage of notifications and emails that you receive every day can negatively impact your creativity. And this particular distraction can be managed. That means putting your phone away! You may feel bored at first, but the wandering mind will soon direct your thoughts.

It may take some getting used to the feeling of idleness if you are accustomed to using social media in your spare time. You don't have to eliminate phone use completely, but to truly allow the default mode network to come online, practice putting your phone away and letting your thoughts roam freely.

You constantly switch between these networks without realizing it throughout your day. However, an awareness of these modes can help to guide your thoughts when you wish to be focused.

Let Your Brain Do The Work For You!

Do you feel creatively stumped? Have you tried every possible method to generate ideas and inspiration to no avail? Perhaps applying your new understanding of the three brain networks might help you generate creative inspiration.

I used to think that I would only come up with ideas if I put all my efforts into brainstorming and doing creative exercises. I tried prompts, free association, timed-interval writing, and more with determined focus and resolve—yet I was seldom happy with the outcome. I would sprint through an idea generation activity only to review the fruits of my labor and criticize what I had come up with. The "inner critic" within me, as it is sometimes called, was inhibiting my creativity.

But it was the same focus—the active executive network—prohibiting me from creating with free-flowing inspiration. The more I tried to hunker down and force out the creativity, the less I was able to do so. There is a difference between idea generation and idea evaluation. It can be hard to distinguish between the two if you have an active inner critic criticizing your ideas as you engage creatively. Deep creative focus can mean that idea evaluation sneaks in without you even noticing.

By activating the executive network, my mind was constantly evaluating my ideas instead of creating without judgment. After learning about how brain networks work, I understood that I actually needed to let my brain wander and engage in background processes in order to experience effortless creativity.

I began to let my mind wander as part of my creative process and also built time into my creative schedule to take breaks. I made efforts not to check my phone during my creative time and noticed that my mind was able to wander much more easily than it did before. Sometimes, I even came up with a great idea while just sitting with my thoughts.

Now, I'm not saying that there is no space for brainstorming activities and writing prompts. These techniques can be very helpful in the creative process. It is the *approach* to these techniques that needs to change. Instead of forcing yourself to complete activities, engage with them in a light and playful way. Don't be afraid to sit and let your mind wander until an interesting idea comes your way.

In addition, do your best to reduce the distractions in your environment to make sure that your salient mode network isn't redirecting your attention to stimuli around you. If you have kids, chances are that the noise of their activities is constantly tugging at your attention.

Realistically, it's impossible to reduce all stimuli in your environment. Sometimes the best you can do might be to put in earplugs and move to a location with minimal visual distractions.

There is a time for idea evaluation, but it doesn't come until long after you have been able to engage in meaningful creation. The worst that can happen if you allow yourself the freedom to create without simultaneous evaluation is that you end up not using the idea later on!

Action Steps

1. Pick one of the five habits that can improve brain neuroplasticity and commit to trying one every day for one week. Your chances of success will increase if you hold yourself accountable by doing the activity with someone. Ask a friend or family member if they would be

willing to try the activity with you. After one week, record how this experiment has changed your mindset. What did you learn from the experience?

2. Try consciously identifying which brain network is activated throughout your day. Notice yourself lost in thought during your lunch break? Or, later on, intensely focused on a task before a deadline? Take note of how often these brain states change. Of course, this will likely mean that you're switching between networks by being more conscious of them!

3. Practice sitting with your thoughts for ten uninterrupted minutes. This activity isn't meditation: Allow your thoughts to roam wherever they would like. After ten minutes, write down where your thoughts went. Are you surprised by the direction? Did you notice any unexpected connections or new ideas? Did you feel bored for any amount of time?

Moving On

Because of her young age, Amelie is able to quickly pick up several languages at speeds that her mother cannot possibly keep up with. Amelie may be unaware of how neuroplasticity and the brain networks are helping her rapidly pick up new knowledge and skills, but these processes are always at work in the background. These same processes allow her to generate creative ideas and write short stories.

Once she learns about neuroplasticity and the brain networks, Francine modifies her lifestyle to encourage new neural pathways and learning. She continues attending language classes and also challenges herself to read more in her target and native language and tries to learn new skills as often as she can.

Learning to hone your creativity is undeniably challenging, even when you are aware of your brain's processes. In the next chapter, we will discuss common barriers to creativity and techniques to address these barriers.

Chapter Summary

- Neuroplasticity refers to neurons in your brain creating new networks and strengthening existing networks. Your brain is the most neuroplastic in childhood, but you can encourage its function in adulthood as well.
- Your brain activity increases when you engage in stimulating activities. Adopting habits that stimulate your brain will improve its function.
- The three major brain networks are the default mode network, the executive network, and the salience network. The DMN is active when you are mentally at rest while the executive network is at work when you are actively focused on a task or goal. The salient network monitors

stimuli in your environment and regulates your emotional response to stimuli.

- By understanding the three brain networks, you can work on using them to your creative advantage by taking breaks and reducing distractions in your environment.

7

WHAT HOLDS BACK YOUR ARTISTIC SPARK?

SPOTLIGHTING THE CHALLENGES TO THE HUMAN CREATIVE PROCESS

What's The One Unifier For All Creatives?

If there is one thing that all creative people have in common, it's probably the inability to create! That's right. At some point or another, every creative is going to encounter a barrier to their creativity that makes it feel impossible to create.

These barriers can be material, such as lack of a creation space for activities that require dedicated spaces, financial hardship, or even responsibilities such as kids or an ill family member. However, barriers to creativity can also be more abstract: mental blocks, exhaustion, mental illness, and lack of motivation can all be barriers to creativity.

You might feel blocked by your inability to break unhelpful habits, unable to change your perspective on a problem or project, lack motivation, or face emotional challenges. All of these blocks can affect your creativity and make it difficult for you to find joy in projects you want to do.

You've almost certainly experienced at least one of these barriers to creativity. If you haven't, I would be shocked! But the good news about barriers to creativity is that, because they are so common, there are so many techniques and solutions to resolve them.

Many people will identify work as the primary thief of creativity. Almost an equal number will cite work as the primary source of their creativity. According to Mihaly Csikszentmihalyi, people who find fulfillment at work "tend to experience their jobs ... as completely integrated with the rest of their lives" (p. 61).[1] A disconnect between work and the rest of your life can constitute a huge barrier to your creativity.

I have personally gone through multiple stretches of time where my creative capacity is close to zero. Sometimes the duration of time is as long as several years. As a student working multiple part-time jobs, I found the workload overwhelming. I barely had time to complete basic household tasks let alone find time to be creative.

At a certain point, I had resigned myself to the reality that my creative days were gone. I just didn't have that *spark* that allowed me to create. My notebooks, filled with old writing, collected dust on my bookshelf. Every so often, I would leaf through them, remember the fervent joy of creation, and long to return to those times when words seemed to leap onto the page from my pen.

I seemed to re-prove this theory every time I tried, unsuccessfully, to write. Instead, I thought of all the assignments I needed to complete and how I should be spending my time on something more beneficial than writing. The words did not come.

I can tell you that even if you feel like you will never be able to be creative again, it is possible.

In this chapter, we will discuss the biggest barriers to creativity and how to identify these obstacles in your life. At times when I felt that I could never be creative ever again, I failed to see how my circumstances were preventing me from accessing my creativity.

The first step to overcoming obstacles to your creativity is simply being able to identify what your particular challenges are.

Material Barriers

As mentioned, sometimes the barriers to creativity can be the material circumstances of your life. If you work more than one job, you likely lack the time (and energy!) to be creative. Material barriers can be any external factor that inhibits your creativity, from social pressures to lack of time or resources.

It would be lovely if we could plan and schedule our creativity to occur in neat intervals in short periods: the half-hour lunch break at work, the free hour that you have between your evening tasks and bedtime, or the chunk of time on Saturday mornings before your children return from soccer practice. But realistically, we can't always make these times work.

Even if you try, one of your coworkers might sit beside you at lunch to have a conversation. You might be so exhausted before bed that all you have the mental capacity for is watching an episode of a sitcom. Saturday mornings might be the only uninterrupted time you have to complete essential house chores. Life just *gets in the way*.

Those with children would surely say that their children's well-being, safety, and happiness are prioritized over finding the time and resources to be creative. Especially when children are in their infancy, parents have a near-constant responsibility to their children, which eats up virtually all free time and attention.

These kinds of obstacles are material barriers: obstacles to your creativity that have to do with the non-negotiables in life such as work, family obligations, and lifestyle upkeep and maintenance.

Social pressures may also be a material barrier to your creativity. This may look like a spouse or partner who is not supportive of your creative endeavors, unable to see why they are important to you. It may also look like the residual emotions of an upbringing in which you were told that being creative is a waste of time. Both barriers can have lasting impacts on your ability to access time, materials, or space to be creative.

Another common material barrier to creativity is money. It's true—any creative pursuits have few financial requirements (to write, you need only a pen and paper; to dance, you need only the physical capability of your body and a reasonably sized space to move). Yet just as often, creative pursuits *do* require financial investment. A painter needs not only a few basic brushes but also the primary colors, which, being finite resources, must be periodically replaced as they run out. Of course, you can obtain budget materials relatively easily, but even these costs will add up if you are a prolific painter.

Financial barriers can be especially problematic if you plan to use your creativity in any professional capacity. Yes, to write you may only need a pen and paper, but nowadays to submit your creations for publication, you need access to a word processing application and a device to type with such as a computer, laptop, or phone. Though these items are quite common at the time of writing, I do not wish to ignore those who still do not have access to these resources.

Similarly, a dancer in a troupe may be required to purchase a special uniform for shows if not also for rehearsals. A painter can go quite far with even the most basic materials but achieving certain compositions or techniques will eventually require more specialized tools.

There are numerous material barriers that a creative person may face, even if they want more than anything to be creative. These material barriers are real, significant challenges to being creative, and finding ways around them can be extremely difficult.

The next chapter will discuss some possible solutions to these common barriers to creativity, but in this chapter, I encourage you to think about the material barriers to your creativity. Often, because they are inescapable facts of life, people struggle to identify how they impact creativity. But the first step to addressing these barriers is identifying where they show up for you.

Mental Barriers

Another type of barrier to creativity is a mental barrier. Being more abstract than material barriers, they can be more difficult to identify. A classic example of a mental barrier is artist's block (also known as writer's block), the feeling that your mind is too blank or too cluttered, thus preventing you from being creative.

However, other kinds of mental barriers include being too distracted, laziness, lack of direction or purpose, functional fixedness (only being able to see how something is conventionally used or thought of), self-censorship or criticism, micromanagement, overthinking, and fear of rejection.

Mental barriers can occur when all the other conditions for creativity are met, but you still cannot engage in meaningful creativity. For example, maybe your creative space is clean, quiet, and equipped with everything you need to engage in a creative activity. Yet, you find that you continuously become distracted or cannot find the motivation to create anything.

In your case, if laziness is a barrier to creating, you may feel like you have no drive to produce anything. This barrier might occur if you do not see any purpose in being creative or would always prefer to engage in a low-effort activity such as watching a movie.

Another extremely common mental barrier is self-criticism and censorship. Self-criticism and censorship happen when you are in the process of creation and have nagging thoughts such as "this work is terrible; it has no value," "no one will ever want to see or read this," and "I can't possibly depict this idea because of what others will think." These kinds of thoughts can occur when you evaluate the products of your creation too early in the process. We touched on this idea in Chapter 6 as a result of the executive mode network being over-activated.

Similarly, overthinking occurs when you cannot meaningfully create because you are too caught up in thoughts about planning or perfection. I am often unable to be creative for this reason, finding that I overthink each word or pen stroke to the point where I cannot create at all.

You may be familiar with the feeling of creating a first draft of a project and becoming overwhelmed by the possibility that others will laugh at or ridicule what you have created. This feeling, which can be thought of as fear of rejection, may stop you from continuing a creative project or prevent you from starting it at all.

Finally, a mental barrier may be as simple as forming a habit in which you avoid being creative. Perhaps you fell out of a routine where you carved out creative time and are now you are having trouble returning to your practice.

There are as many possibilities for mental barriers as people in the world. You might resonate with several of these mental barriers or even come up with different ones that you experience. You may even find that you face both material and mental barriers to creativity.

As with the material barriers, we will discuss possible remedies to these common creativity barriers in the next chapter, but in the meantime, take note of which mental barriers seem familiar to you and which barriers you experience the most often.

Action Steps

1. Write down as many material barriers to your creativity as you can identify. Consider work responsibilities, family obligations, financial difficulties, social pressures, and anything else you can think of. Did you consider these to be barriers to creativity before reading this chapter?

2. Write down as many mental barriers to your creativity as you can identify. What mental processes stop you from being meaningfully creative? Do you have a harsh inner critic? Do you find yourself easily distracted? Do you lack motivation, purpose, or drive to be creative?

3. Which of these barriers do you consider to be unchangeable or unresolvable, and why?

Moving On

For many years, I could not even recognize my own experiences with barriers to creativity, instead believing that I had lost my creative spark forever. Material barriers such as work took up so much time that I did not have the energy to be creative. I felt that they were an unchangeable fact of life that I needed to accept.

It wasn't until years later that I accidentally rediscovered my ability to be creative. This discovery came from trying an entirely new creative activity and becoming completely immersed in the experience of creating! Though I had felt so creatively hopeless for so long, I eventually found joy in creating again, not only in my newfound creative activity but also in the act of writing.

Though I may have reignited my creative spark accidentally, there are many things you can do to address your personal barriers to creativity and take steps to handle them. In the next chapter, we will tackle these barriers to creativity by discussing strategies and techniques for reducing or eliminating these barriers entirely.

Chapter Summary

- *Every* creative person will experience barriers to their creativity at some point in their lives. Sometimes it can be difficult to even identify these obstacles to creativity.
- There are two types of barriers to creativity: material barriers to do with your life's circumstances and mental barriers which stem from your thoughts and inner experiences.
- Barriers to creativity can be anything from lack of time, and responsibility for children, to fear of rejection.

8

SUSTAINING THE CREATIVE FLAME

HOW TO DEAL WITH ROADBLOCKS TO KEEP THE FIRES OF CREATIVITY BURNING

Claudia Borrows A Book

On the day of her 18th birthday, Claudia moves out of the small Texas town where she grew up to New York City with only one suitcase of clothes. No, she didn't have Broadway ambitions, but she had always been drawn to the city and wanted to take a gap year to work and save up for college in the city where she had always dreamed of living.

She takes a minimum-wage waitressing job that just barely covers her rent, food, and utilities. Mostly, she's content with this lifestyle but also quite bored. Her restaurant shifts are mostly in the evening, leaving her several hours of time in the day to fill despite not knowing anyone else in the city besides her roommates.

Claudia's one creative passion is video recording and editing. Since her move, she's used an old camcorder to capture footage on the streets of New York but has no way to edit them, having broken her computer the previous year.

Unable to afford a new computer, Claudia keeps recording until her memory card fills up. Even with the tips she makes at work, it'll take months of saving before she can buy a computer. After finally eating up the last bit of storage space on her memory card, Claudia knows that she needs to find something else to do in her free time. She decides to visit the public library, follow the advice of her mother, and read a book.

Truthfully, she has not willingly visited a library since middle school. She feels like a fish out of water as she moves through the stacks trying to find something interesting to read. She settles on a non-fiction title about filmmaking and heads to the checkout.

By some stroke of luck or perhaps even clairvoyance, the librarian scanning the title seems to sense her interest in film production.

"You know, we have recording equipment available for rent on the third floor and all of the computers in the media section have editing software free for people who have a library card," the librarian says, grinning at Claudia's amazed expression.

Claudia has always been under the impression that libraries were only for book borrowing. She thanked the librarian and backtracked up to the media section with her library card, logging in to the first computer she saw.

It wasn't state-of-the-art software, but it was everything that she needed to edit her footage.

The library became a daily destination for Claudia, who could not believe that the library offered this for *free*.

Many barriers to creativity, such as the financial barrier that Claudia faces, have equally creative solutions. Of course, not every barrier will have an easy solution. Claudia, for instance, has an excess of time and no major responsibilities other than work, factors that allow her to use the library's resources in her creative practice.

For you, things may be more complicated. Addressing barriers to creativity can be mentally overwhelming and even draining. When facing barriers to creativity, our connection with consciousness and spirit plays a key role in overcoming them. Beyond the surface level, many of the barriers to creativity have deep-rooted beliefs about why we *can't* overcome adversity.

Moving past the mental wall of limiting concepts, those false beliefs that reside in the subconscious and harm your ability to change your circumstances, can give you the strength to change mental or material barriers to your creativity.

Solutions To Material Barriers

If you are like Claudia and experience financial barriers to your creative practice, there are potential solutions to access space, equipment, and other materials to enable your creative practice.

These suggestions may not reflect the resources available in your particular community or location. If possible, do some research about the resources and support in your city of residence.

<u>Libraries And Community Resources</u>

Libraries offer a multitude of resources for free to the public that go beyond borrowing books and media. Libraries often offer access to computers and other electronic devices, cameras and video equipment, online repositories of movies, software for editing and word processing, (audio)books, music, databases of information, and even audio recording space. Your library might even offer free classes or events catering to creative activities and often provide free supplies as part of these events.

You may also have a community center in your vicinity with cheap or free space rentals, classes, and resources that you can access. They sometimes offer dance classes, pottery workshops, or arts and crafts nights. These community centers often have bulletin boards where you can find out about other events and workshops in your community. These events are often free to the public and can be a great place to engage in a creative activity with others in your community.

Universities and colleges also tend to offer some workshops and events that are open to the public. Look into events at your local campus that offer free entry and supplies provided for attendees. If the need for space is one of your creative barriers, these events can be a great way to access space for free. You might even make a friend or two!

Online Selling Platforms And Callouts

You'd be surprised how many people out there have old or unused art supplies that they are looking to get rid of. Tons of people buy supplies thinking they will like an activity, only to abandon the new hobby just as quickly. Or, others receive art supplies as gifts during the holidays that never get used. Common art supplies and other equipment such as markers, pens, pencil crayons, paint and paint brushes, canvases and sketchbooks, tools, clay, swimsuits, ice skates, printers, stationary, and even specialty items may be kicking around in someone's storage.

Search platforms like Craigslist and Facebook Marketplace for your desired items. If you can't find what you're looking for, write a callout post on your social media or selling platform to see if anyone has the supplies you want that they could donate to you. People often don't realize that items they've been meaning to throw out for years could actually be used by someone else.

You might also find message boards or online groups where people post items they no longer want for free. See if your community has a local "Buy Nothing" group and inquire if anyone is willing to part with old supplies or equipment. Sometimes these platforms operate on a trading basis for items not listed for free, so you may be able to leverage things you already have or skills to trade for your desired items.

Find Second-Hand Materials

If you can't find your supplies or equipment for free in your community, you may be able to obtain them with some luck at a thrift store or charity shop. Most second-hand stores have a craft supply section where you can find everything from stamps and ink to unopened sets of pencil crayons. In the sports section, you might be able to find swimsuits, unitards, and ice-skating gear. It may take some digging, but sometimes you can be surprised at what you find.

If you live in an urban center, your city might even have a dedicated second-hand craft and art store that sells discounted supplies. Stores like this are a treasure trove of supplies at a fraction of the cost, meaning that you might be able to access materials that would be otherwise inaccessible to you.

For others, barriers to creativity may be due to time and energy rather than financial need. Whether it is because of work, being a parent, or other life responsibilities, scarcity of time can have a significant impact on your ability to be creative.

Your individual circumstances are unique. No two people have the same responsibilities and resources! As such, it's impossible to predict your personal situation accurately and provide relevant advice. The following points are suggestions for removing or reducing material barriers to being creative, but you will likely need to come up with strategies tailored to your distinct needs.

Meet Yourself Where You're At Right Now

If your goal is to work on your creative endeavor once a week, but you can only manage about once a month, maybe maintaining your current level of commitment is enough. Sometimes, responsibilities split between work and family can take up virtually all of your time. These things are important! Though they might get in the way of your ability to be creative, it might be the case that there is nothing that you can do to reduce those time commitments at the present moment. It's better to accept that you can only commit one block of time a month to being creative than not doing anything at all until you're at a point where your desired goal is attainable.

Ask For Help

It's easier said than done, but asking those around you for help with your responsibilities might free up some time for you to dedicate to creativity. This point may be especially useful if you have children but can't afford to have a babysitter or put them in daycare. If you can't find time to create because you always need to be watching your kids, you could ask another parent that you know if they would be interested in taking turns watching the kids on a daily or monthly schedule. Your kids will be happy because they get to spend more time with friends, which frees up time for you to create. Even asking family and friends could help you relieve your responsibilities—you'd be surprised just how often people are happy to help when they know it will allow you to spend time doing something that you're passionate about.

Make Creativity A Private Practice

If you face social pressures that inhibit your creativity, a solution may be more complicated than simply talking to those who don't support your creative practice. Cultural and social attitudes run deep and can be extremely difficult to change. Instead, devise plans for a solitary creative practice if this is the case for you. If possible, try engaging in your creative practice when others are not in your home or having an outside destination (cafe, park, library, or other public space) where you can go to be creative. You don't have to share your work with anyone.

Addressing material barriers to creativity realistically can be difficult and sometimes impossible. Even if there is nothing that you can do right now to change your circumstances, be patient and focus on what you can do to open up possibilities for creative capacity later on.

Solutions To Mental Barriers

Trying to be creative when you are facing a mental obstacle can feel like having an argument with yourself. Removing mental barriers isn't as simple as deciding that you want to create, a reality that I'm sure you are familiar with if you've ever tried unsuccessfully to remedy a mental barrier to creativity.

How, then, can you help restore your creativity? Let's discuss what you can do to revitalize your creativity. As always, take what works and leave what doesn't—not every technique or idea will work for you.

Implement Some Structure

If you have a continuing art practice or personal project, following exercises that develop your personal taste might prompt you to explore new ways of seeing. If you feel directionless in your art practice, structuring your time around a set of exercises or prompts may provide some much-needed structure. For example, if you like to draw but never know what you should draw, develop a list of prompts (there are lots of great ones you can find online!) and challenge yourself to draw one prompt every time you engage in your practice. This structure will help you get a sense of your personal artistic style and the kinds of things you like to create.

Another way to do this is implementing scheduling into your routine. You might schedule specific time slots for certain tasks in your creative process or define concrete goals for how much you want to create in a period. People tend to be polarized about scheduling their creative time—for some, it works really well, and for others, it is completely unhelpful!

Use A Reversal Technique

Reversal technique is changing how you think about a situation to shift your perspective and approach it with fresh eyes. Classically, reversal techniques ask you to shift around the wording in a question to change how you approach answering it. This technique is great if you are stuck on a specific problem or question. For example, if your question is "how can *my book* gain *readers' interest?*" the reversal would be "how can *readers' interest* gain *my book?*" Switching the wording of the question in this case reframes it so that there isn't a presumed scarcity of attention. Suddenly, the question is now about how readers who have an existing interest can access your book instead of being about the problem of generating inexistent attention.

Reframing Questions

Similar to the reversal technique, reframing questions ask you to shift your focus from a negative point of view to a positive one, though with this activity, you are *generating* questions rather than rephrasing existing ones. To try this technique, ask yourself the following questions: What might be a different way to look at this situation? How could you view this challenge as an opportunity? What can you learn from this experience? How might this situation benefit you in the long run? What are some positive aspects of this situation that you haven't considered?

Asking reframing questions can shift your mindset from being stuck to viewing the challenge at hand as an opportunity to learn, grow, or develop in a way you might not have if the solution was clearer.

Breaking The Invisible Barrier Of Assumptions

Much like assuming that the readers of your book are approaching your writing with no existing interest, many creatives have unspoken assumptions about their work that inhibit their creativity. This might be the case for you if you believe (consciously or subconsciously) that your work isn't good enough, you don't have original ideas, or that creativity should feel easy. All of these assumptions will impact your ability to be creative!

Ask yourself what assumptions you have about your work that might be limiting your creativity. The first step to unlearning them is recognizing them and then challenging their truthfulness. Use reframing questions to do this: what if my work *is* good enough? What if my ideas *are* original? What if creativity *can* feel difficult?

Tap Into The Subconscious Mind

If you're overthinking your work or creative process, try intentionally letting go of all expectations by engaging in intense focus time where you create without allowing your thinking mind to criticize or process what you are creating.

Your subconscious formulates ideas in an environment free of censorship or judgment. Nancy Andreasen describes this jumbled idea-generation process as a "primordial soup" where "the unconsciousness and process of making connections must arise from the efforts of the association cortex."[1] In other words, the subconscious mind generates connections between images and concepts to create ideas that are entirely new.

Your subconscious mind is a powerful tool for creative practice. Allow yourself to create messily, imperfectly, and mindlessly. This process will allow your subconscious mind to come forward. In this state, you might be surprised by what you create.

Observation And Mindfulness

Sometimes, creative inspiration is lurking around us when we're too distracted to even notice it! If your mental block has to do with a lack of inspiration, practicing intentional observation and mindfulness may help you. Try to be surprised by something every day or notice something creative done by someone else. For example, sitting in a public space for an hour watching people pass by will yield countless fascinating interactions. Alternatively, seek out creative projects by other artists that you wouldn't normally encounter. Attend a gallery event, poetry reading, local theater production, or another activity in your area that you would not normally have attended.

Curiosity And Interest

It may seem obvious, but following your curiosities and interests can renew your creative spark. When something strikes a spark of interest, follow it. Don't censor. Don't limit yourself to what you think is possible or reasonable.

Aim For Complexity

If you're finding your creative routine redundant or boring and that is what is getting in the way of being creative, try increasing the complexity of your practice. Set up a challenge or feat that raises the difficulty of the activity or alter something about your process. For instance, if you are right-handed, it might be an interesting challenge to see what you can create using only your left hand. Or, you could try drawing something with your eyes closed! Experiments like these ones can yield unexpected results and inspire creativity through the unexpected.

Divergent Thinking

Divergent thinking refers to approaching a singular problem with a multitude of ideas.[2] The idea is to break away from conventional ideas and open up new possibilities or solutions. If you find yourself stuck on something, divergent thinking could help you move past the block. One activity to help you engage in divergent thinking is creating a mind map where you take a piece of paper (or use a whiteboard or digital surface), write your problem in the middle, and write ideas and thoughts that branch out from the main problem. The more you can generate, the better. Once you've exhausted your ideas, take a look at the map and try to find connections between the ideas to help you envision solutions or ways forward.

These suggestions are certainly not definitive ways to move past barriers to creativity. Rather, they should serve as a starting point to experiment with what works for you so that you can engage in further research and learning.

Action Steps

- Spend some time reflecting on your unique barriers to creativity and possible short-term or long-term solutions. What steps can you realistically take to reduce or remove your barriers to creativity? What resources do you have around you that you can access?
- Try any three of the suggestions mentioned in this chapter. Which ones worked well for you? Which ones did not? If none of the three that you tried worked well for you, keep experimenting until you find one that does.
- Ask a friend or family member what they think inhibits you creatively. Sometimes, we're so close to the task at hand that we can't see the bigger picture. Asking for an outside opinion might reveal something that you had not considered.

Moving On

For Claudia, addressing the material barrier of financial difficulty meant accessing a resource in her community that provided the tools that she needed for her practice. For you, it might mean something completely different.

There's a good chance that it will involve multiple strategies and resources to help you resolve the barriers to your creativity. Use this chapter as a starting point for developing your personal strategy.

In the next chapter, we will discuss how you can not only engage with your creative practice but also *cultivate* creativity in your life.

Chapter Summary

- The barriers to creativity in your life will be specific to your circumstances. They could involve a mix of both material and mental barriers.
- You may need to experiment with different strategies, methods, and techniques for removing barriers to creativity in your life. Failure is part of the process! If one solution does not work for you, consider it part of the learning process and keep trying new things.
- Don't be afraid to ask those around you for help. Sometimes, having an outside perspective can reveal something that you had not considered about yourself or your creativity.

9

THE CREATIVE EDGE

HOW TO CULTIVATE AN ARTISTIC SENSITIVITY THAT ALIGNS WITH LIFE'S GOALS AND AMBITIONS

O ptimal creativity is almost synonymous with pleasure, but incorporating it into your life might feel like a lot more pain than pleasure.

Struggling with maintaining the presence of creativity in your life can lead to you feeling unfulfilled, uninspired, or even purposeless. Those who feel called to an artistic practice, craft, movement, or skill can feel lost if they cannot engage with the activity regularly. This is the importance of cultivating creativity in your life.

Savannah, a full-time graphic designer with a hobby painting practice on the side, has all of the time, resources, and energy to be creative, yet she still can't seem to get around to painting most of the time. Often, she gets home from her day job and by the time she eats dinner, finds herself turning on the TV and spending her evenings binge-watching reality shows instead of doing the creative activity that she loves.

She's not really sure why she is having so much trouble getting herself to be creative. She's got lists of future projects she wants to make, countless tubes of paint and brushes, and enough time during her week that she's been finishing multiple seasons of her favorite dating show every week. And further, this activity has become the new normal for her after work. She finds comfortable routines like these hard to break.

The thing is that Savannah expects that her creative time will just *happen* effortlessly. Everything will line up perfectly and one day she'll just feel motivated to begin painting and the image will flow out of her paintbrush almost like magic. But this moment never happens.

Savannah is fed up with herself. Why can't she just do the thing she supposedly loves to do? Sure, maybe her artist's corner has been messy for months and she hasn't really made time to reflect on what she would like to get out of her creative practice... but does that have that much of an impact on the ability to create?

It would be great if our creativity *did* just effortlessly occur without needing to change anything about our lives. But in reality, creativity needs to be cultivated.

Step One: Get Your Priorities Straight

Let's use Savannah's dilemma as a case study for how you can cultivate creativity in your life. It's normal for your periods of creativity to wax and wane, but if you're in a bit of a rut like Savannah, you can take a few steps to invite creativity back into your life.

The first thing you can do to ease back into being creative is to set intentions around your practice. Setting intentions really can change the outcome of your desires. The desire to do something only has the potential to influence whether you take action, whereas setting intention has more direct control over your actions.[1]

Cultivating a creative mindset can start with mindfulness, the intentional process of creating awareness of our surroundings and ourselves. By being mindful, we develop a greater understanding of our desires and goals in life and can use this information to take logical steps to get to that point.

Savannah decides that setting intentions will help her realize her creative goals. She knows that reestablishing her creative practice will take time, so these intentions will evolve over time to fit her needs. To start, she decides to set three simple and attainable intentions:

1. Clean up and organize her art-making space.

2. Reflect on what has been stopping her from creating art for the last few months.

3. Complete two small paintings next week.

Savannah's intentions set a goalpost for where her creativity can begin again. These intentions are actionable and measurable so that she has a clear understanding of how she needs to proceed. Also, she understands that her intentions need space to evolve as time goes on.

Much like New Year's resolutions, you do need to back up your intentions with actions, or else they will never end up coming into being! Yet setting these intentions as concrete goals or objectives can get the ball rolling and increase your motivation. I recommend writing these intentions down on a physical piece of paper and keeping it in an area that will remind you of the intentions you set.

For example, Savannah may choose to hang up her intentions on the wall in her artist's space. She also put a copy on her fridge so that each day when she got home from work, she would see her intentions and remind herself of the steps she promised herself she would take.

Step Two: Do Something About It

Savannah begins with her first actionable goal: to clean up her space. Over the last few months, random items were piled up in the space that she used to paint, making the space difficult to use. Savannah *hates* cleaning. Sure, no one really likes to clean up, but for her, it was such a tedious chore that she could not bring herself to do it. As a result, her space had become really cluttered and neglected.

She had also stored her painting supplies in a way that made them difficult to access. She resolved to spend a couple hours on the weekend tidying up the space and making her art supplies more functional. Even this one change improved her motivation to start painting again.

Taking the time to shape your space in a way that works for you will make creating in your surroundings much more doable. Living in a space that you find over-cluttered, visually unappealing, or not functional can impact the amount of creativity that you can have in your life. For Savannah, the clutter in her art-making space made the prospect of creating more difficult because there was a direct obstacle in the way. In order to be able to use the space, she needed to set aside some time to reorganize it and clear away the clutter.

You may have a similar problem with the space you have dedicated to creativity. Or perhaps you don't have any space at all dedicated to creativity. If this is the case, even setting aside a small nook for creativity can help create a divide in your space and get you into a creative state of mind. If you don't have space for an entire desk or table, consider a small folding table that you can easily store when not in use.

Step Three: Reflect And React

Savannah's next step is to reflect on what's been stopping her from being able to create. She spends fifteen minutes writing about the challenges she's been facing at work and how the exhaustion 0f her day-to-day life, though manageable, has been leading to an avoidance of her creative pursuits. After this reflection, she recognizes the need for active rest to be able to focus on her creative practice.

No one is at their creative best when they are exhausted and burned out. Allowing yourself time to rest and opportunities to reflect on and ponder your experience will open the door to more creativity. Finding time for rest and creativity means taking a close look at your time commitments and responsibilities.

To cultivate your creativity, you may need to take charge of your schedule. It may be the case that you have the time to create in theory, but in practice, you always end up agreeing to a social event or taking the easy route and curling up to watch TV every day. Taking charge of your schedule means committing to time spent being creative, even if it means sometimes saying no to a social function or resisting the ability to just sit down and zone out to a show.

I'm not saying that you should *never* do these things. Making time for your social life and relaxation is essential for a healthy lifestyle. But if you plan to use your Thursday evenings to write a novel, you need to schedule your social life and relaxation time around this commitment. Treat creative time like an important meeting that you cannot change. Intentionally setting the expectation that you will create during that time—and then actually sticking to it—will form a strong habit.

Step Four: Find Balance

Finally, a crucial component of cultivating your creativity is figuring out what you like and what you hate about life and how to balance these two aspects. Start doing more of what you love and less of what you hate. For Savannah, this meant taking a real look at her disdain for cleaning and figuring out ways to reduce the time she spends doing it, while also making sure that her space is functional for creativity. Making sure that cleaning was out of the way actually made more time for her to do what she loves: painting.

And so that's what Savannah does next. She paints two pieces the week after setting the intentions and even ends up working on a third because the act of painting again brought her another great idea for a piece. She ends up revisiting her intentions to readjust, setting new challenges for herself now that she has been able to clear up her space and reestablish her connection to creativity.

Cultivating creativity in your life is an ever-changing but continuous process. Reevaluate your goals and intentions regularly to ensure your creative practice aligns with your goals and ambitions.

Action Steps

- Come up with three actionable steps for improving the quality of your creative time.

Consider your needs regarding space, time, and energy. How will you remind yourself of these goals? How will you keep yourself accountable?

- Find a friend or family member who has similar creative goals to you. Share your intentions with each other and offer suggestions for how they can best meet their goals. How can you help each other to cultivate creativity? Are there steps you can take together? This may mean planning time together such as a weekly creativity session where you work independently on your projects in the same space. Pairing up with a buddy makes staying accountable to your goals much more achievable!

- Consider keeping a blog, journal, or social media account where you document your creative journey. Document works in progress, challenges, failures, successes, and experiments. Abandon the idea that what you produce in these records needs to be good–it's about establishing consistency and intentionality with your creativity. Seeing your progress over time will motivate you to continue regularly engaging with your chosen creative activity.

Moving On

If you are like Savannah, there might not be anything in the way of your creative practice except for the work of cultivating your creativity. It's incredibly easy to fall into a pattern of behavior that doesn't involve creativity. Being creative is like a muscle: If you stop using it long enough, it weakens and this might make you feel defeated. But like a muscle, slow and steady progress will rebuild its strength to the same, if not higher, levels.

If you're re-establishing your relationship with creativity after a long period of disuse, go easy on yourself! Consistency and patience will bring you the results that you're looking for.

A great way to start that work is through activities and exercises to engage your creativity. The final chapter of this book will provide more exercises, activities, and questions for you to cultivate your creativity.

Chapter Summary

- Even if you have all the time, space, and resources you need to be creative, you will still need to intentionally cultivate your creativity.
- Building a strong connection to your sense of creativity will take time and effort; if you've fallen into the habit of avoiding the work of being creative, be patient but consistent to rebuild your creative practice.
- Taking small steps like setting intentions or goals for your creative practice can pave the way for quality creative time. To be effective, these

intentions and goals should always be backed by action.

- To have the best success with regularly practicing creativity, make sure that you are well rested, have a tidy space to be creative, and that your activity brings you genuine pleasure.

10

CHALLENGE YOUR CREATIVE CAPACITY

PRAGMATIC DRILLS TO TEST YOUR ARTISTIC
WITS AND STRENGTHEN YOUR CREATIVITY

Y ou've almost made it to the end of this book,
which shows an incredible commitment to being
creative. So, now what? You might have learned
a lot in the process of reading this book, but maybe you
haven't yet made any real-life changes or steps to improve
your creative capacity. That's what this chapter is for.

This chapter will offer necessary exercises and activities to
put into practice the lessons you've learned in this book.
You might be tempted to just skim through and do them
in the future, but I implore you to *take the time right now* to
do even one of these exercises in full. Yes, you could
promise yourself that you will get to them later, but more
often than not, later never comes; this is why doing them
right now is imperative.

You can apply the following exercises to pretty much any
creative practice. I encourage you to try as many of them
as possible, but to start, just pick one and see where it

takes you. Approach these exercises with playful and light energy—they're meant to stoke your creative energy, not suck it away!

#1: The Anti-Perfection Game

For this game, the objective is the opposite of most: I want you to lose. Only by losing can you win this game. Confused yet?

If you are a perfectionist, this one is definitely for you. Sometimes, we can become so caught up in our expectations and visions of what we want to create that we become too obsessed with the end result of creativity rather than how it feels to create in the moment. The objective of this game is to focus entirely on the process and forget the outcome altogether.

It's so rare that we are allowed to fail. At work, or in relationships, we are expected to strive for excellence and are generally held to a high standard. This activity is meant to allow you to shed those expectations and see what it's like to create without any of those rules.

For this game, you'll need to spend seven days doing art badly. Terribly, even. I want you to make the worst art that you possibly can. You're aiming for anti-perfection; bad art on purpose.

You can dance badly, sing badly, write badly, carve badly, cook badly, or do any other activity as long as it's done badly. Try to lose yourself in the process of creating itself and rejoice in the freedom to create without caring about the final product.

What's the worst that can happen? You don't ever have to let these creations see the light of day. In fact, you can even burn or destroy them after the seven days are up.

You can do the same activity every day or try something else each day. For example, you could paint badly for seven days straight or find a different activity to do badly on each of the seven days.

After you've done your creative activity badly for seven days, reflect on the experience either in your head or in writing. What fears came up as you were creating? Did anything end up being a lot better than you expected? How did it feel to permit yourself to create badly?

#2: Everything's Better With A Friend (Or Many Friends!)

This activity is a collaborative one. If you are in a creative rut or simply want to find new ways to motivate yourself to be creative, doing a creative activity with another person (or a group of people) is a great way to do this.

Organize a creativity night with a friend or group of friends where you all engage in the same creative activity. You could host one of the following: a collage night where everyone cuts bits and pieces from magazines and newspapers; an embroidery night where everyone embroiders fabric of their choice; a dance night where you all choreograph a routine together; or even a photography walk in the park, where everyone takes photos of each other and the nature that you encounter.

Get creative with your ideas and ask your friends for suggestions on what they would like to do. Building a creative community can help deepen your connections and inspire unique ideas.

You could also try a variation of this activity where each individual engages in a different creative activity, based on a theme or concept that you set. For instance, you could choose the theme of "marine life" and each of your friends could bring an activity of their choice. You might end up with paintings of whales, sculptures of starfish, illustrations of a coral reef, and more! The beauty of this variation is that everyone will approach the theme differently, and you'll have a great time sharing your creations with your friends.

#3: Back To School (Kind Of)

Learning, as discussed in Chapter 6, is extremely beneficial to developing your creativity. For this activity, I'm challenging you to go back to school. Take a class, course, or workshop where you are challenged to learn something new. You might learn an entirely new skill or a new technique in an area that you are already familiar with.

If you are a painter who works mainly with acrylics, you could find a course in a language you don't know. You could also find an advanced workshop teaching watercolor or oil painting techniques. This activity aims to expand your existing knowledge, whether it is within your domain or in a completely new one.

Check out offerings in your local area for ideas on what you could learn. Some typical classes that I have seen include learning to sew and knit, workshops in poetry and prose, cooking classes, language classes, metalworking and woodworking, improv classes, comedy workshops, singing lessons, photography workshops, gardening tutorials, and various dance classes. You can find a course offering for almost anything.

Community centers often offer tons of courses at affordable rates, but you can also find offerings at your local college or university. Sometimes private academics offer courses and classes that may interest you.

Learning online definitely counts. There are amazing learning channels on YouTube and platforms like Masterclass and Skillshare. If you don't have access to any in-person learning in your area or can't afford to take a class, online learning is a great opportunity to learn something new from the comfort of your home or on a budget.

#4: A Fun Kind Of Test

This activity will help you figure out what kind of creative you are. It is much like one of those quizzes you used to find in magazines matching you with a celebrity based on your interests and desires in a partner. But instead, the results will match you with the type of creative person you are!

Select the best answer for each question and keep track of your answers as you go along.

Question 1: Which Of The Following Most Applies To You?

1. You're great with your hands
2. You like to experiment
3. You find that your mind is always wandering
4. You enjoy solving complex puzzles
5. You wish you could capture the essence of the world around you

Question 2: Your Friends Would Describe You As...

1. Handy with tools and having practical skills
2. Obsessed with understanding the world around you
3. Always in your own world
4. Extremely logical and rational
5. Someone who notices the beauty in everything

Question 3: You Spend Most Of Your Free Time...

1. Making physical objects and decorations
2. Trying new ways of doing things out of curiosity
3. Daydreaming about the future or the fantastical

4. Performing calculations and estimates for original designs of buildings, vehicles, cities, or other contraptions
5. Processing your experiences by creating visual representations

Question 4: In Your Daily Life, You Tend To Like...

1. A mix of straightforward tasks and time to think
2. Predictability with room for surprise
3. Novelty
4. Routines and structure
5. Unstructured time

Question 5: How Do You Handle Criticism?

1. You take it to heart and feel discouraged
2. You use it as motivation to improve your work
3. You try to ignore it and focus on your own vision
4. You become defensive and argumentative
5. You try to understand the other point of view

Question 6: What Inspires You The Most?

1. Inventions and useful items
2. The laws of physics
3. Emotions and feelings
4. Order and reason
5. Other people

Question 7: How Do You Approach Problem-Solving?

1. I try to think outside the box and use what I have around me
2. I try many different approaches with trial and error
3. I rely on my intuition and gut feelings
4. I take a logical and analytical approach
5. I reflect and approach with curiosity

Results

If you selected mostly As, you're a **Crafty Type**. You're great at making things with your hands and love when what you produce has a practical use while also being aesthetically pleasing. They love turning the old into the new and re-envisioning existing things as something entirely new. Crafty types are resourceful and quick to pick up new skills. They don't mind putting in lots of time to yield the desired results.

If you selected mostly Bs, you're a **Scientific Type**. You're fascinated by the world around you and eager to test its limits and observe what you see around you. Scientific types don't mind failure; they understand that it is a crucial step to revealing the truth.

If you selected mostly Cs, you're an **Imaginative Type**. Complex worlds and intricate storylines exist in your head, and you have the talent to bring them to life. There are no bounds to your creativity, and you are fiercely independent and protective of your ideas. Sometimes others can't see your vision until it has come to fruition. Imaginative types delight in considering the infinite possibility of each day.

If you selected mostly Ds, you're a **Mathematical Type**. Ever logical and grounded, you're often not the first person that people think of as creative. To you, creativity happens in calculated steps, reasoned methods, and becoming the master of all rules so that you can manipulate them to your liking. You have the determination and persistence to work through tough problems even when it feels like the solution is impossible.

If you selected mostly Es, you're an **Artistic Type**. You capture the beauty and whimsy of everyday life and process your subjectivity through your craft. You love observing others and the natural world and take great inspiration from them. You always try to filter the world around you through your experience and perspective. You enjoy being left to your own devices and letting your creativity take you to unexpected places.

If you happen to have a tie between your selections, you may have an overlap between the types. You could be Scientific-Imaginative, Crafty-Artistic, or Imaginative-Artistic. In this case, you take elements from both types and have a unique mix of creative attributes.

#5: Game-ify Your Creativity

If you remember from the "How To Hack Your Brain To Improve Creativity" chapter, games can improve your creativity by challenging you to think differently about a situation.

For this exercise, I challenge you to bring the principles of games into your creative practice. No matter your chosen creative pursuit, *make it into a game* in whatever way you would like.

This may sound confusing at first, but part of the challenge here is using your creativity (ha!) to figure out how your creative activity could become the basis for a game.

I'll give you an example to help you get started. Let's say that your chosen creative practice is writing. You might come up with fifty random words and phrases and write them on flashcards. Then your challenge is to select a card at random and speed write for five minutes about that prompt.

Say you pick a card with the word **flexible**. You set a timer and immediately start writing whatever comes to mind. At the end of the five minutes, you've produced a wacky micro story about a tiger who joins the circus! These stories are meant to be fun and promote quick thinking and playfulness in your creative practice.

You can game-ify your creativity to be a solo or shared activity. Have fun with this activity and don't be afraid to change the rules and come up with multiple variations of your game!

#6: An Impractical Ritual

For this activity, you will create an elaborate creative ritual. I'm talking *way* over the top, time-consuming, unnecessary ritual steps. An **impractical ritual**, if you will.

Even though this activity might feel purposeless or unnecessary, developing patterns and routines can habituate you to being creative regularly rather than only spontaneously.

Forming a ritual can help you create a Pavlovian effect on yourself where doing the steps can prime your mind for entering the creative space. The more elaborate the ritual, the longer your mind has to enter the creative space.

However, in this case, this isn't a ritual to be done *every* time you want to be creative. This one is for when you have the time and energy to devote to making your creative session maximally pleasurable and focused.

You should develop a ritual that is filled with things that you like, but here is an example of a creative ritual to get your ideas flowing:

- Tidy your creativity space and arrange any materials you will need during your creative time. Take care with the process.

- Brew a beverage of choice to consume during your creative time. Be intentional and slow with the preparation of your beverage.
- Write down a few intentions for your creative time, whether to let go of expectations, meet a certain tangible goal, or engage for a set amount of time.
- Set up music that helps you get into a creative flow. For you, it might be jazz music, lo-fi beats, classical piano, or upbeat techno.
- Adjust your lighting. Depending on your activity, you might want to dim or brighten the lights or light a scented candle to set the mood.
- Gear up to start creating by moving your body. Select a particular song you can dance to freely or do a mindful yoga practice. Perhaps even a short walk or run.
- Take deep breaths to center yourself and initiate your creative focus.
- Launch into your creative activity.

I recommend having a more minimal ritual to use on a regular basis, but an elaborate ritual can make the creative process feel more intuitive and natural. Plus, it can help if you're going through a creative block. Pull out this ritual next time you're struggling to be creative.

#7: Dress The Part

What would someone stereotypically wear to perform your chosen creative activity? Wear it. Wear it the next time you engage in the activity, no matter where you are or who is around.

If you're a ballet dancer, you may normally rehearse in the comfiest of your dance clothing unless you're performing in front of an audience. For this activity, I want you to

This activity varies in difficulty depending on your creative practice. For example, I am a writer. What do writers wear? Don't they just wear normal clothes like everyone else? I would venture to say yes, there isn't a defined writer's uniform. But if I consider what a writer looks like in our cultural imagination, I might picture a bespeckled person decked out in a tweed jacket and corduroy. Someone who looks like they've just taught an English class or stepped out of the Beinecke library.

Is there a high likelihood that you exclusively write in your comfiest sweatpants and hoodie or a comparable outfit? *Yes.* The point of this exercise is to make the experience feel novel. It might feel silly or like you're wearing a costume, but performance is part of changing the mental state that you are in. *Feeling* like you are someone that would engage in your chosen creative practice.

Chapter Summary

- Applying your knowledge by participating in these relevant exercises will strengthen your commitment to improving your creativity.
- Starting with one of these exercises will get the ball rolling, but make sure to refer back to this book and complete them all to achieve the best results.
- Strengthening your creativity should be approached with playfulness: incorporate games, friends, and fun activities to have a positive mental association with creativity.

AFTERWORD

That you picked up this book in the first place probably means that you already considered yourself a creative person or someone with the capacity for creativity. You may have resonated with stories like that of Tammy, the engineer who didn't consider her work to be creative; Anthony, the woodworker who had lost touch with his creative passion; Francine, the mother inspired by her daughter's creativity; or any of the other's whose stories we touched on. Creativity is a near-universal part of humanity that innately exists within us.

If you've made it this far, there is a good chance that you've already started taking steps to improve your creativity. You might be thinking, now what? I've read this entire book and it's unclear where to go from here.

By now, it is cliché, but the next step is of course *to just go out and create*. That's always going to be the best thing that you can do for your creative capacity.

Another thing that you can do is review the Action Steps at the end of each chapter and Chapter 10: Exercises and resolve to complete each of them. You might have already done so, but chances are that you just kept reading after finishing each chapter. (It's okay, I would do the same!) Now is the time to put the action steps… well, into action. The good news is that you already have this book, which isn't going anywhere. Refer back to it as much as you need and as often as you need.

Completing these action steps will come with a lot of trial and error. Many of the activities might not work with your particular creative style. Yet that's part of their use; finding out what *doesn't* work for you is just as important as finding out what does. I recommend keeping a record of each activity that you complete and some reflections or notes on the experience.

What did you learn about yourself by doing the activity?

Will the experience change how you approach your creative practice, or did it solidify one of your habits or routines?

Did the activity give you any ideas for further reading or exercises you could do next time?

What you do next is up to you, but I hope that what you've learned throughout this book will have a lasting impact on how you engage with the world creatively, no matter your chosen activity or field.

And remember—everything that you need to be creative is already within you.

YOUR LAST CHANCE FOR OUR LIMITED DEAL

DID YOU LIKE WHAT YOU READ? THEN YOU'RE GOING TO LOVE THE FOLLOWING EXCLUSIVE OFFER...

In general, around 50% of the people who start reading do not finish a book. You are the exception, and we are happy you took the time.

To honor this, we invite you to join our exclusive Wisdom University newsletter. You cannot find this subscription link anywhere else on the web but in our books!

Upon signing up, you'll receive two of our most popular bestselling books, highly acclaimed by readers like yourself. We sell copies of these books daily, but you will receive them as a gift. Additionally, you'll gain access to two transformative short sheets and enjoy complimentary access to all our upcoming e-books, completely free of charge!

This offer and our newsletter are free; you can unsubscribe anytime.

Here's everything you get:

✔ How To Train Your Thinking eBook   ($9.99 Value)
✔ The Art Of Game Theory eBook   ($9.99 Value)
✔ Break Your Thinking Patterns Sheet   ($4.99 Value)
✔ Flex Your Wisdom Muscle Sheet   ($4.99 Value)
✔ All our upcoming eBooks   ($199.80* Value)

Total Value: $229.76

Take me to wisdom-university.net for my free bonuses!

(Or simply scan the code with your camera)

Scan Me

*If you download 20 of our books for free, this would equal a value of 199.80$

THE PEOPLE BEHIND WISDOM UNIVERSITY

Michael Meisner, Founder and CEO

When Michael got into publishing books on Amazon, he found that his favorite topic - the thinking process and its results, is tackled in a much too complex and unengaging way. Thus, he set himself up to make his ideal a reality: books that are informative, entertaining, and can help people achieve success by thinking things through.

This ideal became his passion and profession. He built a team of like-minded people and is in charge of the strategic part and brand orientation, as he continues to improve and extend his business.

Claire M. Umali, Publishing Manager

Crafting books is collaborative work, and keeping everyone on the same page is an essential task. Claire oversees all the stages of this collaboration, from researching to outlining and from writing to editing. In her free time, she writes reviews online and likes to bother her cats.

Sonja Pinto, Writer

Sonja is a writer, printmaker, and avid journaler. Sonja holds two degrees in English Literature and an extensive background in professional communications. She loves podcasts, running, and photography and is always looking for new ways to express herself creatively.

Jevette Brown, Content Editor

Jevette is an editor with a background in copy editing, academic writing, and journalism. With bachelor's degrees in Communications and English and a graduate degree in Legal Studies, Jevette's varied experience provides a valuable perspective for diverse content and audiences. Her priority is helping writers fine-tune their material to display their unique voices best.

Sandra Agarrat, Language Editor

Sandra Wall Agarrat is an experienced freelance academic editor/proofreader, writer, and researcher. Sandra holds graduate degrees in Public Policy and International Relations. Her portfolio of projects includes books, dissertations, theses, scholarly articles, and grant proposals.

Michelle Olarte, Researcher

Michelle conducts extensive research and constructs thorough outlines substantiating Wisdom University's book structure. She graduated from Communication Studies with high honors. Her works include screenplays, book editing, book advertisements, and magazine articles.

Ralph Escarda, Layout Designer

Ralph's love for books prevails in his artistic preoccupations. He is an avid reader of non-fictional books and an advocate of self-improvement through education. He dedicates his spare time to doing portraits and sports.

REFERENCES

1. How To Start Your Creative Pursuit?

1. Merriam-Webster. (n.d.). Creativity. In *Merriam-Webster.com dictionary*. Retrieved December 19, 2022, from https://www.merriam-webster.com/dictionary/creativity
2. Bernier, K. (2021). *Lazy creativity: The art of owning your creativity*. Outskirts Press.
3. Rhodes, M. (1961). An analysis of creativity. *The Phi Delta Kappan, 42*(7), 305–310. http://www.jstor.org/stable/20342603
4. Gauntlett, D. (2022). *Creativity: Seven keys to unlock your creative self*. Polity Press.
5. Runco, M. A., & Jaeger, G. J. (2012). The standard definition of creativity. *Creativity Research Journal, 24*(1), 92–96. https://doi.org/10.1080/10400419.2012.650092
6. Runco, M. A., & Jaeger, G. J. (2012). The standard definition of creativity. *Creativity Research Journal, 24*(1), 92–96. https://doi.org/10.1080/10400419.2012.650092
7. Fletcher, A., & Benveniste, M. (2022). A new method for training creativity: narrative as an alternative to divergent thinking. *Ann. N.Y. Acad. Sci., 1512*(1),29-45. https://doi.org/10.1111/nyas.14763

2. Discover Your Creative Persona

1. Leddy, T. (1990). Is the creative process in art a form of puzzle solving? *Journal of Aesthetic Education, 24*(3), 83–97. https://doi.org/10.2307/3332801
2. Dul, J. et al. (2011). Work environments for employee creativity. *Ergonomics, 54*(1), 12-20, https://doi.org/10.1080/00140139.2010.542833
3. Mehta, R., Zhu, R. (Juliet), & Cheema, A. (2012). Is noise always bad? Exploring the effects of ambient noise on creative cognition. *Journal of Consumer Research, 39*(4), 784–799. https://doi.org/10.1086/665048

4. Wilmer, H. H., Sherman, L. E., & Chein, J. M. (2017). Smartphones and cognition: A review of research exploring the links between mobile technology habits and cognitive functioning. *Frontiers in Psychology*, *8*, 605. https://doi.org/10.3389/fpsyg.2017.00605

3. What's Your Creative Vibe?

1. Dietrich, A. (2019). Types of creativity. *Psychon Bull Rev 26*, 1–12. https://doi.org/10.3758/s13423-018-1517-7
2. Sinnamon, S., Moran, A., & O'Connell, M. (2012). Flow among musicians: Measuring peak experiences of student performers. *Journal of Research in Music Education*, *60*(1), 6–25. http://www.jstor.org/stable/41348849

4. The Tapestry Of Creative Imprint

1. Csikszentmihalyi, M. (2007). *Creativity: Flow and the Psychology of Discovery and Invention*. Harper Collins.

5. Where Intellect Meets Creativity

1. Gardner, H. (2011). *Frames of mind: The theory of multiple intelligences*. Basic Books.
2. Gardner, H. (2011). *Frames of mind: The theory of multiple intelligences*. Basic Books.
3. Kaufman, J. et al. (2005). Bridging generality and specificity: The amusement park theoretical (APT) model of creativity. *Roeper Review*, *27*(3), 158-163, https://doi.org/10.1080/02783190509554310

6. Neural Pathways Of Creativity

1. Rugnetta, M. (2023, January 26). *neuroplasticity*. Encyclopedia Britannica. https://www.britannica.com/science/neuroplasticity
2. Cassilhas, R. C., Tufik, S., & de Mello, M. T. (2016). Physical exercise, neuroplasticity, spatial learning and memory. *Cellular and Molecular Life Sciences*, *73*, 975–983. https://doi.org/10.1007/s00018-015-2102-0

3. Pickersgill, J. W., Turco, C. V., Ramdeo. K., Rehsi, R. S., Foglia S. D., & Nelson, A. J. (2022). The combined influences of exercise, diet and sleep on neuroplasticity. *Front. Psychol., 13*. https://doi.org/10.3389/fpsyg.2022.831819

4. Phillips, C. (2017). Lifestyle modulators of neuroplasticity: How physical activity, mental engagement, and diet promote cognitive health during aging. *Neural plasticity*, Article 3589271. https://doi.org/10.1155/2017/3589271

5. Fischer, S., & Barabasch, A. (2020). Gamification.: A novel didactical approach for 21st century learning. In E. Wuttke, J. Seifried, & H. Niegemann (Eds.), *Vocational education and training in the Age of Digitization: Challenges and opportunities* (1st ed., pp. 89–106). Verlag Barbara Budrich. https://doi.org/10.2307/j.ctv18dvv1c.8

6. Beaty, R. E., Kenett, Y. N., Christensen, A. P., Rosenberg, M. D., Benedek, M., Chen, Q., Fink, A., Qiu, J., Kwapil, T. R., Kane, M. J., & Silvia, P. J. (2018). Robust prediction of individual creative ability from brain functional connectivity. *Proceedings of the National Academy of Sciences, 115*(5), 1087–1092. https://doi.org/10.1073/pnas.1713532115

7. Beaty, R. E., Kenett, Y. N., Christensen, A. P., Rosenberg, M. D., Benedek, M., Chen, Q., Fink, A., Qiu, J., Kwapil, T. R., Kane, M. J., & Silvia, P. J. (2018). Robust prediction of individual creative ability from brain functional connectivity. *Proceedings of the National Academy of Sciences, 115*(5), 1087–1092. https://doi.org/10.1073/pnas.1713532115

7. What Holds Back Your Artistic Spark?

1. Csikszentmihalyi, M. (1996). *Flow and the psychology of discovery and invention*. HarperCollins.

8. Sustaining The Creative Flame

1. Andreasen, N C. (2011). A journey into chaos: Creativity and the unconscious. *Mens Sana Monogr., 9*(1), 42-53. https://www.ncbi.nlm.nih.gov/pmc/articles/PMC3115302/

2. American Psychological Association. (n.d.). Divergent thinking. In *APA dictionary of psychology*. Retrieved April 1, 2023, from https://dictionary.apa.org/divergent-thinking

9. The Creative Edge

1. Thinnes-Elker, F. et al. (2012). Intention concepts and brain-machine interfacing. *Front. Psychology*, *3*(455). https://doi.org/10.3389/fpsyg.2012.00455

DISCLAIMER

The information contained in this book and its components is meant to serve as a comprehensive collection of strategies that the author of this book has done research about. Summaries, strategies, tips and tricks are only recommendations by the author, and reading this book will not guarantee that one's results will exactly mirror the author's results.

The author of this book has made all reasonable efforts to provide current and accurate information for the readers of this book. The author and their associates will not be held liable for any unintentional errors or omissions that may be found.

The material in the book may include information by third parties. Third party materials are comprised of opinions expressed by their owners. As such, the author of this book does not assume responsibility or liability for any third party material or opinion.

Made in the USA
Monee, IL
15 July 2024

61834241R00100